INSTANT VOR'
AIR FRYER UK
COOKBOOK FOR BEGINNERS

1200 Days Of Delicious, Fast And Easy Air Fryer Recipes To Make Drooling

Homemade Meals For Busy People |With Full Colour Pictures

VIRGINIA B. SHIVER

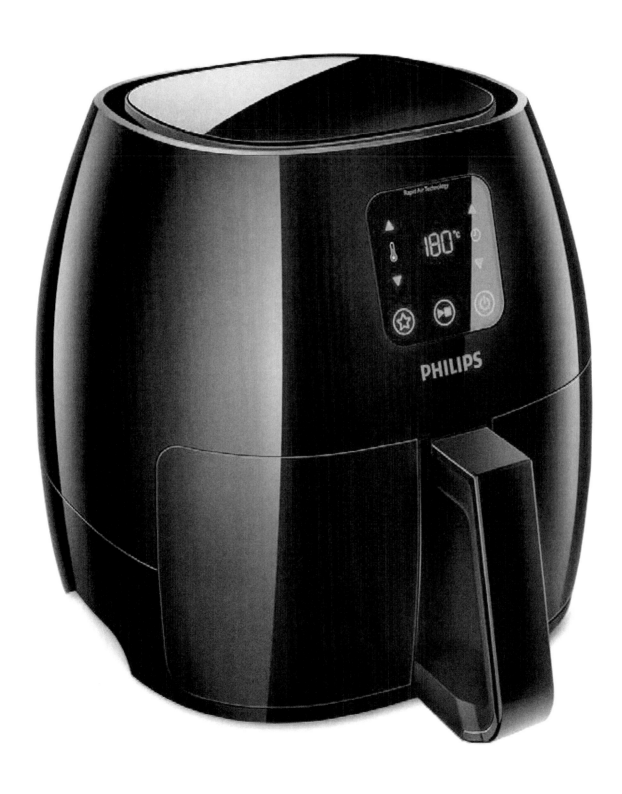

Table of Contents

When we got our first Instant Vortex Air Fryer last year, I was skeptical about it. The premise of the appliance seemed wild to me. However, I kept an open mind and grabbed one. A week later, I was cooking almost everything in my kitchen. While the common conception is that an air fryer is a healthier alternative to a deep fryer, it is much more than that. I have discovered that it has near-limitless potential in my kitchen.

The instant Vortex air fryer is an excellent fit for any kitchen. Now that you have one, the next step is to prepare some delicious meals. This cookbook contains hundreds of possible recipes with readily available ingredients.

Chapter 1 Understanding your Instant Vortex Air Fryer

What can you Do with the Instant Vortex Air Fryer?

The compact design of the Instant Vortex air fryer can be deceiving. You might think that it is just for preparing French fries. However, that is not the case. The Instant Vortex air fryer supports numerous cooking options. These are:

- Air Frying
- Baking
- Broiling
- Dehydrating
- Reheating
- Roasting

The instant Vortex air fryer comes with a powerful fan that circulates heat around your food, which lets you enjoy the same deep-fried food with just a spoonful of oil. Consequently, you can enjoy healthy meals faster.

Instant Vortex air fryers have a wide temperature range of 95 to 400 degrees Fahrenheit and various other customizable functions. It ensures that almost anything you can prepare using other appliances in the kitchen can be made in the air fryer, but much healthier. Additionally, it comes with over-heat protection and an auto-off function to prevent any hazardous accidents in the kitchen.

Easy to Use

One of the reasons why you would consider buying an air fryer is how fast it is to prepare tasty meals. With the instant Vortex air fryer, everything is streamlined to ensure you can prepare your meals as quickly as possible.

It comes with an intuitive control panel, which makes it possible to get everything right on the first try. It features simple, well-labeled buttons. It also comes with an internal audio notification to tell you the various stages of the cooking process. For instance, a mid-way beep tells you when it is time to flip the food. Additionally, it has a built-in light to help you monitor the cooking process without taking out the drawer. In general, this is one of the easiest air fryers to help prepare tasty, healthy meals for the whole family fast.

Who Can Use It?

The Instant Vortex air fryer is a diverse kitchen appliance designed for numerous use cases. A single person that loves to eat home-cooked meals can use it. Everything can be prepared in just a few minutes with minimal effort—a perfect appliance for a family that loves healthy cooking. Whether making snacks or preparing full meals, you will find the air fryer an inseparable part of your home cooking.

Adapted Oven Recipes

If you have always wanted an oven but lack space, this air fryer serves the function quite well. You will find numerous recipes in this cookbook adapted from oven-based recipes. The goal is to ensure that you can enjoy almost any meal for which you would need another appliance at your convenience.

Enjoying home-cooked meals can be delightful with the Instant Vortex air fryer. It no longer has to feel like a complex chore requiring you to set aside hours to prepare meals. With the great recipes in this cookbook, you will enjoy delicious home-cooked meals daily.

Try them out today!

Chapter 2
Breakfast

Mexican Breakfast Pepper Rings

Prep Time: 5 minutes | Cook Time: 10 minutes | Serves 4

- Olive oil
- 1 large red, yellow, or orange bell pepper, cut into four ¾-inch rings
- 4 eggs
- Salt
- Freshly ground black pepper
- 2 teaspoons salsa

1. Lightly spray a small round air fryer–friendly pan with olive oil.
2. Place 2 bell pepper rings on the pan. Crack one egg into each bell pepper ring. Season with salt and black pepper.
3. Spoon ½ teaspoon of salsa on top of each egg.
4. Place the pan in the fryer basket. Air fry until the yolk is slightly runny, 5 to 6 minutes or until the yolk is fully cooked, 8 to 10 minutes.
5. Repeat with the remaining 2 pepper rings. Serve hot.

Cajun Breakfast Muffins

Prep Time: 10 minutes | Cook Time: 10 minutes | Serves 6

- Olive oil
- 4 eggs, beaten
- 2¼ cups frozen hash browns, thawed
- 1 cup diced ham
- ½ cup shredded Cheddar cheese
- ½ teaspoon Cajun seasoning

1. Lightly spray 12 silicone muffin cups with olive oil.
2. In a medium bowl, mix together the eggs, hash browns, ham, Cheddar cheese, and Cajun seasoning in a medium bowl.
3. Spoon a heaping 1½ tablespoons of hash brown mixture into each muffin cup.
4. Place the muffin cups in the fryer basket.
5. Air fry until the muffins are golden brown on top and the center has set up, 8 to 10 minutes.

Hearty Blueberry Oatmeal

Prep Time: 10 minutes | Cook Time: 25 minutes | Serves 6

- 1½ cups quick oats
- 1¼ teaspoons ground cinnamon, divided
- ½ teaspoon baking powder
- Pinch salt
- 1 cup unsweetened vanilla almond milk
- ¼ cup honey
- 1 teaspoon vanilla extract
- 1 egg, beaten
- 2 cups blueberries
- Olive oil
- 1½ teapoons sugar, divided
- 6 tablespoons low-fat whipped topping (optional)

1. In a large bowl, mix together the oats, 1 teaspoon of cinnamon, baking powder, and salt.
2. In a medium bowl, whisk together the almond milk, honey, vanilla and egg.
3. Pour the liquid ingredients into the oats mixture and stir to combine. Fold in the blueberries.
4. Lightly spray a round air fryer–friendly pan with oil.
5. Add half the blueberry mixture to the pan.
6. Sprinkle ⅛ teaspoon of cinnamon and ½ teaspoon sugar over the top.
7. Cover the pan with aluminum foil and place gently in the fryer basket.
8. Air fry for 20 minutes. Remove the foil and air fry for an additional 5 minutes. Transfer the mixture to a shallow bowl.
9. Repeat with the remaining blueberry mixture, ½ teaspoon of sugar, and ⅛ teaspoon of cinnamon.
10. To serve, spoon into bowls and top with whipped topping.

Mini Cinnamon Sticky Rolls

Prep Time: 10 minutes | Cook Time: 25 minutes | Serves 18 rolls

- 2 teaspoons cinnamon
- ⅓ cup light brown sugar
- 1 (9-by-9-inch) frozen puff pastry sheet, thawed
- All-purpose flour, for dusting
- 6 teaspoons (2 tablespoons) unsalted butter, melted, divided

1. In a small bowl, mix together the cinnamon and brown sugar.
2. Unfold the puff pastry on a lightly floured surface. Using a rolling pin, press the folds together and roll the dough out in one direction so that it measures about 9 by 11 inches. Cut it in half to form two squat rectangles of about 5½ by 9 inches.
3. Brush 2 teaspoons of butter over each pastry half, and then sprinkle with 2 generous tablespoons of the cinnamon sugar. Pat it down lightly with the palm of your hand to help it adhere to the butter.
4. Starting with the 9-inch side of one rectangle and using your hands, carefully roll the dough into a cylinder. Repeat with the other rectangle. To make slicing easier, refrigerate the rolls for 10 to 20 minutes.
5. Using a sharp knife, slice each roll into nine 1-inch pieces. Transfer the rolls to the center of the sheet pan. They should be very close to each other, but not quite touching. For neater rolls, turn the outside rolls so that the seam is to the inside. Drizzle the remaining 2 teaspoons of butter over the rolls and sprinkle with the remaining cinnamon sugar.
6. Select BAKE, set temperature to 350°F, and set time to 25 minutes. Select START/PAUSE to begin preheating.
7. Once the unit has preheated, slide the sheet pan into the oven.
8. When cooking is complete, remove the pan and check the rolls. They should be puffed up and golden brown. If the rolls in the center are not quite done, return the pan to the oven for another 3 to 5 minutes. If the outside rolls are dark golden brown before the inside rolls are done, you can remove those with a small spatula before returning the pan to the oven.
9. Let the rolls cool for a couple of minutes, then transfer them to a rack to cool completely.

Bacon Cups

Prep Time: 10 minutes | Cook Time: 30 minutes | Serves 2

- 2 eggs
- 1 slice tomato
- 3 slices bacon
- 2 slices ham
- 2 tsp grated parmesan cheese

1. Preheat your fryer to 375°F/190°C.
2. Cook the bacon for half of the directed time.
3. Slice the bacon strips in half and line 2 greased muffin tins with 3 half-strips of bacon
4. Put one slice of ham and half slice of tomato in each muffin tin on top of the bacon
5. Crack one egg on top of the tomato in each muffin tin and sprinkle each with half a teaspoon of grated parmesan cheese.
6. Bake for 20 minutes.
7. Remove and let cool.
8. Serve!

French Toast Casserole

Prep Time: 10 minutes | Cook Time: 12 minutes | Serves 6

- 3 large eggs
- 1 cup whole milk
- ¼ teaspoon kosher salt or ⅛ teaspoon fine salt
- 1 tablespoon pure maple syrup
- 1 teaspoon vanilla
- ¼ teaspoon cinnamon
- 3 cups (1-inch) stale bread cubes (3 to 4 slices)
- 1 tablespoon unsalted butter, at room temperature

1. In a medium bowl, whisk the eggs until the yolks and whites are completely mixed. Add the milk, salt, maple syrup, vanilla, and cinnamon and whisk to combine. Add the bread cubes and gently stir to coat with the egg mixture. Let sit for 2 to 3 minutes so the bread absorbs some of the custard, then gently stir again.
2. Grease the bottom of the sheet pan with the butter. Pour the bread mixture onto the pan, spreading it out evenly.
3. Select AIR ROAST, set temperature to 350°F, and set time to 12 minutes. Select START/PAUSE to begin preheating.
4. Once the unit has preheated, slide the pan into the oven.
5. After about 10 minutes, remove the pan and check the casserole. The top should be browned and the middle of the casserole just set. If more time is needed, return the pan to the oven and continue cooking.
6. When cooking is complete, serve warm with additional butter and maple syrup, if desired.

Strawberry Toast

Prep Time: 10 minutes | Cook Time: 8 minutes | Serves 4

- 4 slices bread, ½-inch thick
- butter-flavored cooking spray
- 1 cup sliced strawberries
- 1 teaspoon sugar

1. Spray one side of each bread slice with butter-flavored cooking spray. Lay slices sprayed side down.
2. Divide the strawberries among the bread slices.
3. Sprinkle evenly with the sugar and place in the air fryer basket in a single layer.
4. Cook at 390°F for 8 minutes. The bottom should look brown and crisp and the top should look glazed.

Three-Berry Dutch Pancake

Prep Time: 10 minutes | Cook Time: 16 minutes | Serves 4

- 2 egg whites
- 1 egg
- ½ cup whole-wheat pastry flour
- ½ cup 2 percent milk
- 1 teaspoon pure vanilla extract
- 1 tablespoon unsalted butter, melted
- 1 cup sliced fresh strawberries
- ½ cup fresh blueberries
- ½ cup fresh raspberries

1. In a medium bowl, use an eggbeater or hand mixer to quickly mix the egg whites, egg, pastry flour, milk, and vanilla until well combined.
2. Use a pastry brush to grease the bottom of a 6-by-2-inch pan with the melted butter. Immediately pour in the batter and put the basket back in the fryer. Bake for 12 to 16 minutes, or until the pancake is puffed and golden brown.
3. Remove the pan from the air fryer; the pancake will fall. Top with the strawberries, blueberries, and raspberries. Serve immediately.

Banana Bread Pudding

Prep Time: 10 minutes | Cook Time: 20 minutes | Serves 4

- Olive oil
- 2 medium ripe bananas, mashed
- ½ cup low-fat milk
- 2 tablespoons peanut butter
- 2 tablespoons maple syrup
- 1 teaspoon ground cinnamon
- 1 teaspoon vanilla extract
- 2 slices whole-grain bread, torn into bite-sized pieces
- ¼ cup quick oats

1. Lightly spray four individual ramekins or one air fryer–safe baking dish with olive oil.
2. In a large mixing bowl, combine the bananas, milk, peanut butter, maple syrup, cinnamon, and vanilla. Using an electric mixer or whisk, mix until fully combined.
3. Add the bread pieces and stir to coat in the liquid mixture.
4. Add the oats and stir until everything is combined.
5. Transfer the mixture to the baking dish or divide between the ramekins. Cover with aluminum foil.
6. Place 2 ramekins in the fryer basket and air fry until heated through, 10 to 12 minutes.
7. Remove the foil and cook for 6 to 8 more minutes.
8. Repeat with the remaining 2 ramekins.

Chocolate-Filled Doughnut Holes

Prep Time: 10 minutes | Cook Time: 12 minutes | Serves 24

- 1 (8-count) can refrigerated biscuits
- 24 to 48 semisweet chocolate chips
- 3 tablespoons melted unsalted butter
- ¼ cup powdered sugar

1. Separate and cut each biscuit into thirds.
2. Flatten each biscuit piece slightly and put 1 to 2 chocolate chips in the center. Wrap the dough around the chocolate and seal the edges well.
3. Brush each doughnut hole with a bit of the butter and air-fry in batches for 8 to 12 minutes.
4. Remove and dust with powdered sugar. Serve warm.

Sweet Potato-Cinnamon Toast

Prep Time: 5 minutes | Cook Time: 8 minutes | Serves 6-8 slices

- 1 small sweet potato, cut into ⅜-inch slices
- oil for misting
- ground cinnamon

1. Preheat air fryer to 390°F.
2. Spray both sides of sweet potato slices with oil. Sprinkle both sides with cinnamon to taste.
3. Place potato slices in air fryer basket in a single layer.
4. Cook for 4 minutes, turn, and cook for 4 more minutes or until potato slices are barely fork tender.

Walnut Pancake

Prep Time: 5 minutes | Cook Time: 20 minutes | Serves 4

- 3 tablespoons butter, divided into thirds
- 1 cup flour
- 1½ teaspoons baking powder
- ¼ teaspoon salt
- 2 tablespoons sugar
- ¾ cup milk
- 1 egg, beaten
- 1 teaspoon pure vanilla extract
- ½ cup walnuts, roughly chopped
- maple syrup or fresh sliced fruit, for serving

1. Place 1 tablespoon of the butter in air fryer baking pan. Cook at 330°F for 3 minutes to melt.
2. In a small dish or pan, melt the remaining 2 tablespoons of butter either in the microwave or on the stove.
3. In a medium bowl, stir together the flour, baking powder, salt, and sugar. Add milk, beaten egg, the 2 tablespoons of melted butter, and vanilla. Stir until combined but do not beat. Batter may be slightly lumpy.
4. Pour batter over the melted butter in air fryer baking pan. Sprinkle nuts evenly over top.
5. Cook for 20 minutes or until toothpick inserted in center comes out clean. Turn air fryer off, close the machine, and let pancake rest for 2 minutes.
6. Remove pancake from pan, slice, and serve with syrup or fresh fruit.

Fried Eggs

Prep Time: 4 minutes | Cook Time: 3 minutes | Serves 2

- 2 eggs
- 3 slices bacon

1. Heat some oil in a deep fryer at 375°F/190°C.
2. Fry the bacon.
3. In a small bowl, add the 2 eggs.
4. Quickly add the eggs into the center of the fryer.
5. Using two spatulas, form the egg into a ball while frying.
6. Fry for 2-3 minutes, until it stops bubbling.
7. Place on a paper towel and allow to drain.
8. Enjoy!

Scotch Eggs

Prep Time: 10 minutes | Cook Time: 30 minutes | Serves 4

- 4 large eggs
- 1 package Jimmy Dean's Pork Sausage (12 oz)
- 8 slices thick-cut bacon
- 4 toothpicks

1. Hard-boil the eggs, peel the shells and let them cool.
2. Slice the sausage into four parts and place each part into a large circle.
3. Put an egg into each circle and wrap it in the sausage.
4. Place inside your refrigerator for 1 hour.
5. Make a cross with two pieces of thick-cut bacon.
6. Place a wrapped egg in the center, fold the bacon over top of the egg and secure with a toothpick.
7. Cook inside your fryer at 450°F/230°C for 25 minutes.
8. Enjoy!

French Toast Sticks with Strawberry Sauce

Prep Time: 6 minutes | Cook Time: 14 minutes | Serves 4

- 3 slices low-sodium whole-wheat bread, each cut into 4 strips (see Tip)
- 1 tablespoon unsalted butter, melted
- 1 egg
- 1 egg white
- 1 tablespoon 2 percent milk
- 1 tablespoon sugar
- 1 cup sliced fresh strawberries
- 1 tablespoon freshly squeezed lemon juice

1. Place the bread strips on a plate and drizzle with the melted butter.
2. In a shallow bowl, beat the egg, egg white, milk, and sugar.
3. Dip the bread into the egg mixture and place on a wire rack to let the batter drip off.
4. Air-fry half of the bread strips for 5 to 7 minutes, turning the strips with tongs once during cooking, until golden brown. Repeat with the remaining strips.
5. In a small bowl, mash the strawberries and lemon juice with a fork or potato masher. Serve the strawberry sauce with the French toast sticks.

Monkey Bread

Prep Time: 7 minutes | Cook Time: 8 minutes | Serves 4

- 1 (8-ounce) can refrigerated biscuits
- ¼ cup white sugar
- 3 tablespoons brown sugar
- ½ teaspoon cinnamon
- ⅛ teaspoon nutmeg
- 3 tablespoons melted unsalted butter

1. Open the can of biscuits, separate, and cut each biscuit into 4 pieces.
2. Combine the white sugar, brown sugar, cinnamon, and nutmeg in a shallow bowl and mix well.
3. Dip each biscuit briefly into the butter and roll in the sugar mixture to coat. Place in a 6-by-6-by-2-inch baking pan.
4. Bake for 6 to 9 minutes or until golden brown. Let cool for 5 minutes, then serve. Be careful when eating at first, because the sugar gets very hot.

Spinach Eggs and Cheese

Prep Time: 10 minutes | Cook Time: 30 minutes | Serves 2

- 3 whole eggs
- 3 oz cottage cheese
- 3-4 oz chopped spinach
- ¼ cup parmesan cheese
- ¼ cup of milk

1. Preheat your fryer to 375°F/190°C.
2. In a large bowl, whisk the eggs, cottage cheese, the parmesan and the milk.
3. Mix in the spinach.
4. Transfer to a small, greased, fryer dish.
5. Sprinkle the cheese on top.
6. Bake for 25-30 minutes.
7. Let cool for 5 minutes and serve.

Chapter 3
Snacks & Appetizers

Egg Roll Pizza Sticks

Prep Time: 10 minutes | Cook Time: 5 minutes | Serves 4

- Olive oil
- 8 pieces reduced-fat string cheese
- 8 egg roll wrappers
- 24 slices turkey pepperoni
- Marinara sauce, for dipping (optional)

1. Spray a fryer basket lightly with olive oil. Fill a small bowl with water.
2. Place each egg roll wrapper diagonally on a work surface. It should look like a diamond.
3. Place 3 slices of turkey pepperoni in a vertical line down the center of the wrapper.
4. Place 1 mozzarella cheese stick on top of the turkey pepperoni.
5. Fold the top and bottom corners of the egg roll wrapper over the cheese stick.
6. Fold the left corner over the cheese stick and roll the cheese stick up to resemble a spring roll. Dip a finger in the water and seal the edge of the roll
7. Repeat with the rest of the pizza sticks.
8. Place them in the fryer basket in a single layer, making sure to leave a little space between each one. Lightly spray the pizza sticks with oil. You may need to cook these in batches.
9. Air fry until the pizza sticks are lightly browned and crispy, about 5 minutes.
10. These are best served hot while the cheese is melted. Accompany with a small bowl of marinara sauce, if desired.

Cajun Zucchini Chips

Prep Time: 10 minutes | Cook Time: 15 minutes | Serves 4

- Olive oil
- 2 large zucchini, cut into ⅛-inch-thick slices
- 2 teaspoons Cajun seasoning

1. Spray a fryer basket lightly with olive oil.
2. Put the zucchini slices in a medium bowl and spray them generously with olive oil.
3. Sprinkle the Cajun seasoning over the zucchini and stir to make sure they are evenly coated with oil and seasoning.
4. Place slices in a single layer in the fryer basket, making sure not to overcrowd. You will need to cook these in several batches.
5. Air fry for 8 minutes. Flip the slices over and air fry until they are as crisp and brown as you prefer, an additional 7 to 8 minutes.

Greek Street Tacos

Prep Time: 10 minutes | Cook Time: 3 minutes | Serves 8

- 8 small flour tortillas (4-inch diameter)
- 8 tablespoons hummus
- 4 tablespoons crumbled feta cheese
- 4 tablespoons chopped kalamata or other olives (optional)
- olive oil for misting

1. Place 1 tablespoon of hummus or tapenade in the center of each tortilla. Top with 1 teaspoon of feta crumbles and 1 teaspoon of chopped olives, if using.
2. Using your finger or a small spoon, moisten the edges of the tortilla all around with water.
3. Fold tortilla over to make a half-moon shape. Press center gently. Then press the edges firmly to seal in the filling.
4. Mist both sides with olive oil.
5. Place in air fryer basket very close but try not to overlap.
6. Cook at 390°F for 3 minutes, just until lightly browned and crispy.

Mexican Potato Skins

Prep Time: 10 minutes | Cook Time: 55 minutes | Serves 6

- Olive oil
- 6 medium russet potatoes, scrubbed
- Salt
- Freshly ground black pepper
- 1 cup fat-free refried black beans
- 1 tablespoon taco seasoning
- ½ cup salsa
- ¾ cup reduced-fat shredded Cheddar cheese

1. Spray a fryer basket lightly with olive oil.
2. Spray the potatoes lightly with oil and season with salt and pepper. Pierce each potato a few times with a fork.
3. Place the potatoes in the fryer basket. Air fry until fork tender, 30 to 40 minutes. The cooking time will depend on the size of the potatoes. You can cook the potatoes in the microwave or a standard oven, but they won't get the same lovely crispy skin they will get in the air fryer.
4. While the potatoes are cooking, in a small bowl, mix together the beans and taco seasoning. Set aside until the potatoes are cool enough to handle.
5. Cut each potato in half lengthwise. Scoop out most of the insides, leaving about ¼ inch in the skins so the potato skins hold their shape.
6. Season the insides of the potato skins with salt and black pepper. Lightly spray the insides of the potato skins with oil. You may need to cook them in batches.
7. Place them into the fryer basket, skin side down, and air fry until crisp and golden, 8 to 10 minutes.
8. Transfer the skins to a work surface and spoon ½ tablespoon of seasoned refried black beans into each one. Top each with 2 teaspoons salsa and 1 tablespoon shredded Cheddar cheese.
9. Place filled potato skins in the fryer basket in a single layer. Lightly spray with oil.
10. Air fry until the cheese is melted and bubbly, 2 to 3 minutes.

Grilled Cheese Sandwich

Prep Time: 5 minutes | Cook Time: 5 minutes | Serves 2

- 4 slices bread
- 4 ounces Cheddar cheese slices
- 2 teaspoons butter or oil

1. Lay the four cheese slices on two of the bread slices and top with the remaining two slices of bread.
2. Brush both sides with butter or oil and cut the sandwiches in rectangular halves.
3. Place in air fryer basket and cook at 390°F for 5 minutes until the outside is crisp and the cheese melts.

Mozzarella Sticks

Prep Time: 10 minutes | Cook Time: 5 minutes | Serves 4

- 1 egg
- 1 tablespoon water
- 8 eggroll wraps
- 8 mozzarella string cheese "sticks"
- sauce for dipping

1. Beat together egg and water in a small bowl.
2. Lay out eggroll wraps and moisten edges with egg wash.
3. Place one piece of string cheese on each wrap near one end.
4. Fold in sides of eggroll wrap over ends of cheese, and then roll up.
5. Brush outside of wrap with egg wash and press gently to seal well.
6. Place in air fryer basket in single layer and cook 390°F for 5 minutes. Cook an additional 1 or 2 minutes, if necessary, until they are golden brown and crispy.
7. Serve with your favorite dipping sauce.

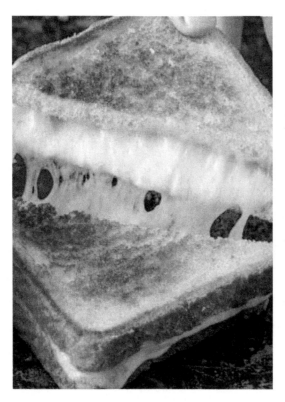

Italian Rice Balls

Prep Time: 25 minutes | Cook Time: 10 minutes | Serves 8 rice balls

- 1½ cups cooked sticky rice
- ½ teaspoon Italian seasoning blend
- ¾ teaspoon salt
- 8 pitted black olives
- 1 ounce mozzarella cheese cut into tiny sticks (small enough to stuff into olives)
- 2 eggs, beaten
- ⅓ cup Italian breadcrumbs
- ¾ cup panko breadcrumbs
- oil for misting or cooking spray

1. Preheat air fryer to 390°F.
2. Stir together the cooked rice, Italian seasoning, and ½ teaspoon of salt.
3. Stuff each black olive with a piece of mozzarella cheese.
4. Shape the rice into a log and divide into 8 equal pieces. Using slightly damp hands, mold each portion of rice around an olive and shape into a firm ball. Chill in freezer for 10 to 15 minutes or until the outside is cold to the touch.
5. Set up 3 shallow dishes for dipping: beaten eggs in one dish, Italian breadcrumbs in another dish, and in the third dish mix the panko crumbs and remaining salt.
6. Roll each rice ball in breadcrumbs, dip in beaten egg, and then roll in the panko crumbs.
7. Spray all sides with oil.
8. Cook for 10 minutes, until outside is light golden brown and crispy.

Jalapeño Poppers

Prep Time: 60 minutes | Cook Time: 5 minutes | Serves 20 poppers

- ½ pound jalapeño peppers
- ¼ cup cornstarch
- 1 egg
- 1 tablespoon lime juice
- ¼ cup plain breadcrumbs
- ¼ cup panko breadcrumbs
- ½ teaspoon salt
- oil for misting or cooking spray
- 4 ounces cream cheese
- 1 teaspoon grated lime zest
- ¼ teaspoon chile powder
- ⅛ teaspoon garlic powder
- ¼ teaspoon salt

1. Combine all filling ingredients in small bowl and mix well. Refrigerate while preparing peppers.
2. Cut jalapeños into ½-inch lengthwise slices. Use a small, sharp knife to remove seeds and veins.
3. For mild appetizers, discard seeds and veins.
4. For hot appetizers, finely chop seeds and veins. Stir a small amount into filling, taste, and continue adding a little at a time until filling is as hot as you like.
5. Stuff each pepper slice with filling.
6. Place cornstarch in a shallow dish.
7. In another shallow dish, beat together egg and lime juice.
8. Place breadcrumbs and salt in a third shallow dish and stir together.
9. Dip each pepper slice in cornstarch, shake off excess, then dip in egg mixture.
10. Roll in breadcrumbs, pressing to make coating stick.
11. Place pepper slices on a plate in single layer and freeze them for 30 minutes.
12. Preheat air fryer to 390°F.
13. Spray frozen peppers with oil or cooking spray. Place in air fryer basket in a single layer and cook for 5 minutes.

Fried Tortellini with Spicy Dipping Sauce

Prep Time: 8 minutes | Cook Time: 20 minutes | Serves 4

- ¾ cup mayonnaise
- 2 tablespoons mustard
- 1 egg
- ½ cup flour
- ½ teaspoon dried oregano
- 1½ cups bread crumbs
- 2 tablespoons olive oil
- 2 cups frozen cheese tortellini

1. In a small bowl, combine the mayonnaise and mustard and mix well. Set aside.
2. In a shallow bowl, beat the egg. In a separate bowl, combine the flour and oregano. In another bowl, combine the bread crumbs and olive oil, and mix well.
3. Drop the tortellini, a few at a time, into the egg, then into the flour, then into the egg again, and then into the bread crumbs to coat. Put into the air fryer basket, cooking in batches.
4. Air-fry for about 10 minutes, shaking halfway through the cooking time, or until the tortellini are crisp and golden brown on the outside. Serve with the mayonnaise.

Crispy Old Bay Chicken Wings

Prep Time: 10 minutes | Cook Time: 15 minutes | Serves 4

- Olive oil
- 2 tablespoons Old Bay seasoning
- 2 teaspoons baking powder
- 2 teaspoons salt
- 2 pounds chicken wings

1. Spray a fryer basket lightly with olive oil.
2. In a large zip-top plastic bag, mix together the Old Bay seasoning, baking powder, and salt.
3. Pat the wings dry with paper towels.
4. Place the wings in the zip-top bag, seal, and toss with the seasoning mixture until evenly coated.
5. Place the seasoned wings in the fryer basket in a single layer. Lightly spray with olive oil. You may need to cook them in batches.
6. Air fry for 7 minutes. Turn the wings over, lightly spray them with olive oil, and air fry until the wings are crispy and lightly browned, 5 to 8 more minutes. Using a meat thermometer, check to make sure the internal temperature is 165°F or higher.

Glazed Chicken Wings

Prep Time: 5 minutes | Cook Time: 25 minutes | Serves 4

- 8 chicken wings
- 3 tablespoons honey
- 1 tablespoons lemon juice
- 1 tablespoon low sodium chicken stock
- 2 cloves garlic, minced
- ¼ cup thinly sliced green onion
- ¾ cup low sodium barbecue sauce
- 4 stalks celery, cut into pieces

1. Pat the chicken wings dry. Cut off the small end piece and discard or freeze it to make chicken stock later.
2. Put the wings into the air fryer basket. Air fry for 20 minutes, shaking the basket twice while cooking.
3. Meanwhile, combine the honey, lemon juice, chicken stock, and garlic, and whisk until combined.
4. Remove the wings from the air fryer and put into a 6 x 2 pan. Pour the sauce over the wings and toss gently to coat.
5. Return the pan to the air fryer and air fry for another 4 to 5 minutes or until the wings are glazed and a food thermometer registers 165°F. Sprinkle with the green onion and serve the wings with the barbecue sauce and celery.

Hollandaise Sauce

Prep Time: 1 minutes | Cook Time: 1 minutes | Serves 8

- 8 large egg yolks
- ½ tsp salt
- 2 tbsp fresh lemon juice
- 1 cup unsalted butter

1. Combine the egg yolks, salt, and lemon juice in a blender until smooth.
2. Put the butter in your microwave for around 60 seconds, until melted and hot.
3. Turn the blender on a low speed and slowly pour in the butter until the sauce begins to thicken.
4. Serve!

Prosciutto-Wrapped Party Pears

Prep Time: 12 minutes | Cook Time: 6 minutes | Serves 8

- 2 large ripe Anjou pears
- 4 thin slices Parma prosciutto (about 2 ounces)
- 2 teaspoons aged balsamic vinegar

1. Peel the pears. Slice into 6 or 8 wedges (depending on the size of the pears) and cut out the core from each wedge.
2. Cut the prosciutto into long strips (one strip per pear wedge). Wrap each pear wedge with a strip of prosciutto. Place the wrapped pears on the sheet pan.
3. Select AIR BROIL, set temperature HIGH, and set time to 6 minutes. Select START/PAUSE to begin preheating.
4. Once the unit has preheated, slide the pan into the oven.
5. After 2 or 3 minutes, check the pears. The pears should be turned over if the prosciutto is beginning to crisp up and brown. Return the pan to the oven and continue cooking.
6. When cooking is complete, remove the pan from the oven. Serve the pears warm or at room temperature with a drizzle of the balsamic vinegar.

Garlic-Parmesan Crunchy Snack Mix

Prep Time: 10 minutes | Cook Time: 6 minutes | Serves 6

- 2 cups oyster crackers
- 2 cups Chex-style cereal (rice, corn, or wheat, or a combination)
- 1 cup sesame sticks
- 8 tablespoons unsalted butter, melted
- ⅔ cup finely grated Parmesan cheese
- 1½ teaspoon granulated garlic
- ½ teaspoon kosher salt or ¼ teaspoon fine salt

1. Place the oyster crackers in a large bowl. Add the cereal and sesame sticks. Drizzle with the butter and sprinkle on the cheese, garlic, and salt. Toss to coat. Place the mix on the sheet pan in an even layer.
2. Select AIR ROAST, set temperature to 350°F, and set time to 6 minutes. Select START/PAUSE to begin preheating.
3. Once the unit has preheated, slide the pan into the oven.
4. About halfway through cooking, remove the pan and stir the mixture. Return the pan to the oven and continue cooking.
5. When cooking is complete, the mix should be lightly browned and fragrant. Let cool. The mixture can be stored at room temperature in an airtight container for 3 to 4 days.

Mini Chicken Meatballs

Prep Time: 10 minutes | Cook Time: 20 minutes | Serves 16 meatballs

- 2 teaspoons olive oil
- ¼ cup minced onion
- ¼ cup minced red bell pepper
- 2 vanilla wafers, crushed
- 1 egg white
- ½ teaspoon dried thyme
- ½ pound ground chicken breast (see Tip)

1. In a 6-by-2-inch pan, mix the olive oil, onion, and red bell pepper. Put the pan in the air fryer. Cook for 3 to 5 minutes, or until the vegetables are tender.
2. In a medium bowl, mix the cooked vegetables, crushed wafers, egg white, and thyme until well combined
3. Mix in the chicken, gently but thoroughly, until everything is combined.
4. Form the mixture into 16 meatballs and place them in the air fryer basket. Air-fry for 10 to 15 minutes, or until the meatballs reach an internal temperature of 165°F on a meat thermometer. Serve immediately.

Vegetable Shrimp Toast

Prep Time: 15 minutes | Cook Time: 6 minutes | Serves 4

- 8 large raw shrimp, peeled and finely chopped (see Tip)
- 1 egg white
- 2 garlic cloves, minced
- 3 tablespoons minced red bell pepper
- 1 medium celery stalk, minced
- 2 tablespoons cornstarch
- ¼ teaspoon Chinese five-spice powder
- 3 slices firm thin-sliced no-sodium whole-wheat bread

1. In a small bowl, stir together the shrimp, egg white, garlic, red bell pepper, celery, cornstarch, and five-spice powder. Top each slice of bread with one-third of the shrimp mixture, spreading it evenly to the edges. With a sharp knife, cut each slice of bread into 4 strips.
2. Place the shrimp toasts in the air fryer basket in a single layer. You may need to cook them in batches. Air-fry for 3 to 6 minutes, until crisp and golden brown. Serve.

Pesto Bruschetta

Prep Time: 10 minutes | Cook Time: 8 minutes | Serves 4

- 8 slices French bread, ½ inch thick
- 2 tablespoons softened butter
- 1 cup shredded mozzarella cheese
- ½ cup basil pesto
- 1 cup chopped grape tomatoes
- 2 green onions, thinly sliced

1. Spread the bread with the butter and place butter-side up in the air fryer basket. Bake for 3 to 5 minutes or until the bread is light golden brown.
2. Remove the bread from the basket and top each piece with some of the cheese. Return to the basket in batches and bake until the cheese melts, about 1 to 3 minutes.
3. Meanwhile, combine the pesto, tomatoes, and green onions in a small bowl.
4. When the cheese has melted, remove the bread from the air fryer and place on a serving plate. Top each slice with some of the pesto mixture and serve.

Homemade Mayonnaise

Prep Time: 5 minutes | Cook Time: 25 minutes | Serves 4

- 1 large egg
- Juice from 1 lemon.
- 1 tsp dry mustard
- ½ tsp black pepper
- 1 cup avocado oil

1. Combine the egg and lemon juice in a container and let sit for 20 minutes.
2. Add the dry mustard, pepper, and avocado oil.
3. Insert an electric whisk into the container.
4. Blend for 30 seconds.
5. Transfer to a sealed container and store in your refrigerator.

Granny's Green Beans

Prep Time: 5 minutes | Cook Time: 5 minutes | Serves 4

- 1 lb green beans, trimmed
- 1 cup butter
- 2 cloves garlic, minced
- 1 cup toasted pine nuts

1. Boil a pot of water.
2. Add the green beans and cook until tender for 5 minutes.
3. Heat the butter in a large skillet over a high heat. Add the garlic and pine nuts and sauté for 2 minutes or until the pine nuts are lightly browned.
4. Transfer the green beans to the skillet and turn until coated.
5. Serve!

Mini Pepper Poppers

Prep Time: 5 minutes | Cook Time: 5 minutes | Serves 4

- 8 mini sweet peppers
- ¼ cup pepper jack cheese, shredded
- 4 slices sugar-free bacon, cooked and crumbled
- 4 oz. full-fat cream cheese, softened

1. Prepare the peppers by cutting off the tops and halving them lengthwise. Then take out the membrane and the seeds.
2. In a small bowl, combine the pepper jack cheese, bacon, and cream cheese, making sure to incorporate everything well
3. Spoon equal-sized portions of the cheese-bacon mixture into each of the pepper halves.
4. Place the peppers inside your fryer and cook for eight minutes at 400°F. Take care when removing them from the fryer and enjoy warm.

Chapter 4
Chicken and Poultry

Mexican Sheet Pan Dinner

Prep Time: 10 minutes | Cook Time: 15 minutes | Serves 4

- 1 pound boneless, skinless chicken tenderloins, cut into strips
- 3 bell peppers, any color, cut into chunks
- 1 onion, cut into chunks
- 1 tablespoon olive oil, plus more for spraying
- 1 tablespoon fajita seasoning mix

1. In a large bowl, mix together the chicken, bell peppers, onion, 1 tablespoon of olive oil, and fajita seasoning mix until completely coated.
2. Spray a fryer basket lightly with olive oil.
3. Place the chicken and vegetables in the fryer basket and lightly spray with olive oil.
4. Air fry for 7 minutes. Shake the basket and cook until the chicken is cooked through and the veggies are starting to char, an additional 5 to 8 minutes.

Parmesan-Lemon Chicken

Prep Time: 1 hour 10 minutes | Cook Time: 20 minutes | Serves 4

- 1 egg
- 2 tablespoons lemon juice
- 2 teaspoons minced garlic
- ½ teaspoon salt
- ½ teaspoon freshly ground black pepper
- 4 boneless, skinless chicken breasts, thin cut
- Olive oil
- ½ cup whole-wheat bread crumbs
- ¼ cup grated Parmesan cheese

1. In a medium bowl, whisk together the egg, lemon juice, garlic, salt, and pepper. Add the chicken breasts, cover, and refrigerate for up to 1 hour.
2. In a shallow bowl, combine the bread crumbs and Parmesan cheese.
3. Spray a fryer basket lightly with olive oil.
4. Remove the chicken breasts from the egg mixture, then dredge them in the bread crumb mixture, and place in the fryer basket in a single layer. Lightly spray the chicken breasts with olive oil. You may need to cook the chicken in batches.
5. Air fry for 8 minutes. Flip the chicken over, lightly spray with olive oil, and cook until the chicken reaches an internal temperature of 165°F, for an additional 7 to 12 minutes.

Creole Cornish Hens

Prep Time: 10 minutes | Cook Time: 40 minutes | Serves 4

- 2 tablespoons olive oil, plus more for spraying
- ½ tablespoon Creole seasoning
- ½ tablespoon garlic powder
- ½ tablespoon onion powder
- ½ tablespoon freshly ground black pepper
- ½ tablespoon paprika
- 2 Cornish hens

1. Spray a fryer basket lightly with olive oil.
2. In a small bowl, mix together the Creole seasoning, garlic powder, onion powder, pepper, and paprika.
3. Pat the Cornish hens dry and brush each hen all over with the 2 tablespoons of olive oil. Rub each hen with the seasoning mixture.
4. Place the Cornish hens in the fryer basket. Air fry for 15 minutes. Flip the hens over and baste with any drippings collected in the bottom drawer of the air fryer. Lightly spray them with olive oil.
5. Air fry for 15 minutes. Flip the hens back over and cook until a thermometer inserted into the thickest part of the thigh reaches at least 165°F and it's crispy and golden, an additional 5 to 10 minutes.
6. Let the hens rest for 10 minutes before carving.

Italian Chicken and Veggies

Prep Time: 10 minutes | Cook Time: 30 minutes | Serves 4

- ¾ cup balsamic vinaigrette dressing, divided
- 1 pound boneless, skinless chicken tenderloins
- Olive oil
- 1 pound fresh green beans, trimmed
- 1 pint grape tomatoes

1. Place ½ cup of the balsamic vinaigrette dressing and the chicken in a large zip-top plastic bag, seal, and refrigerate for at least 1 hour or up to overnight.
2. In a large bowl, mix together the green beans, tomatoes, and the remaining ¼ cup of balsamic vinaigrette dressing until well coated.
3. Spray the fryer basket lightly with oil. Place the vegetables in the fryer basket. Reserve any remaining vinaigrette.
4. Air fry for 8 minutes. Shake the basket and continue to cook until the beans are crisp but tender, and the tomatoes are soft and slightly charred, an additional 5 to 7 minutes.
5. Wipe the fryer basket with a paper towel and spray lightly with olive oil.
6. Place the chicken in the fryer basket in a single layer. You may need to cook them in batches.
7. Air fry for 7 minutes. Flip the chicken over, baste with some of the remaining vinaigrette, and cook until the chicken reaches an internal temperature of 165°F, an additional 5 to 8 minutes.
8. Serve the chicken and veggies together.

Gochujang Chicken Wings

Prep Time: 15 minutes | Cook Time: 25 minutes | Serves 4

- 2 pounds chicken wings
- 1 teaspoon kosher salt
- 1 teaspoon black pepper or gochugaru (Korean red pepper)
- 2 tablespoons gochujang (Korean chile paste)
- 1 tablespoon mayonnaise
- 1 tablespoon toasted sesame oil
- 1 tablespoon minced fresh ginger
- 1 tablespoon minced garlic
- 1 teaspoon sugar
- 1 teaspoon agave nectar or honey
- 1 teaspoon sesame seeds
- ¼ cup chopped scallions

1. For the wings: Season the wings with the salt and pepper and place in the air-fryer basket. Set the air fryer to 400°F for 20 minutes, turning the wings halfway through the cooking time.
2. Meanwhile, for the sauce: In a small bowl, combine the gochujang, mayonnaise, sesame oil, ginger, garlic, sugar, and agave; set aside.
3. As you near the 20-minute mark, use a meat thermometer to check the meat. When the wings reach 160°F, transfer them to a large bowl. Pour about half the sauce on the wings; toss to coat (serve the remaining sauce as a dip).
4. Return the wings to the air-fryer basket and cook for 5 minutes, until the sauce has glazed.
5. Transfer the wings to a serving platter. Sprinkle with the sesame seeds and scallions. Serve with the reserved sauce on the side for dipping.

Hawaiian Huli Huli Chicken

Prep Time: 10 minutes plus marinating| Cook Time: 15 minutes | Serves 4

- 4 boneless, skinless chicken thighs (about 1½ pounds)
- 1 (8-ounce) can pineapple chunks in juice, drained, ¼ cup juice reserved
- ¼ cup soy sauce
- ¼ cup sugar
- 2 tablespoons ketchup
- 1 tablespoon minced fresh ginger
- 1 tablespoon minced garlic
- ¼ cup chopped scallions

1. Use a fork to pierce the chicken all over to allow the marinade to penetrate better. Place the chicken in a large bowl or large resealable plastic bag.
2. Set the drained pineapple chunks aside. In a small microwave-safe bowl, combine the pineapple juice, soy sauce, sugar, ketchup, ginger, and garlic. Pour half the sauce over the chicken; toss to coat. Reserve the remaining sauce. Marinate the chicken at room temperature for 30 minutes, or cover and refrigerate for up to 24 hours.
3. Place the chicken in the air-fryer basket. (Discard marinade.) Set the air fryer to 350°F for 15 minutes, turning halfway through the cooking time.
4. Meanwhile, microwave the reserved sauce on high for 45 to 60 seconds, stirring every 15 seconds, until the sauce has the consistency of a thick glaze.
5. At the end of the cooking time, use a meat thermometer to ensure the chicken has reached an internal temperature of 165°F.
6. Transfer the chicken to a serving platter. Pour the sauce over the chicken. Garnish with the pineapple chunks and scallions.

Sweet and Sour Chicken

Prep Time: 10 minutes | Cook Time: 10 minutes | Serves 6

- 1½ pounds boneless, skinless chicken breasts, cut into 1-inch chunks
- ¾ cup Asian-Style Sauce
- 2 tablespoons ketchup
- 2 tablespoons brown sugar
- 2 tablespoons rice vinegar
- 1 red bell pepper, cut into 1-inch chunks
- 1 green bell pepper, cut into 1-inch chunks
- 6 scallions, cut into 1-inch pieces
- Cooking oil spray
- 1 cup (¾-inch chunks) fresh or canned, drained pineapple

1. Place the chicken in a large bowl. Add the Asian-Style Sauce, ketchup, brown sugar, vinegar, red and green peppers, and scallions. Toss to coat.
2. Spray the sheet pan with cooking oil spray and place the chicken and vegetables on the pan.
3. Select AIR ROAST, set temperature to 375°F, and set time to 10 minutes. Select START/PAUSE to begin preheating.
4. Once the unit has preheated, slide the pan into the oven.
5. After 6 minutes, remove the pan from the oven. Add the pineapple chunks to the pan and stir. Return the pan to the oven and continue cooking.
6. When cooking is complete, remove the pan from the oven. Serve with steamed rice, if desired.

Curried Chicken and Sweet Potatoes

Prep Time: 10 minutes | Cook Time: 20 minutes | Serves 4

- 1 pound boneless, skinless chicken thighs
- 1 teaspoon kosher salt or ½ teaspoon fine salt, divided
- ¼ cup unsalted butter, melted
- 1 tablespoon curry powder
- 2 medium sweet potatoes, peeled and cut in 1-inch cubes
- 12 ounces Brussels sprouts, halved

1. Salt the chicken thighs with ½ teaspoon of kosher salt. Place them in the center of the sheet pan.
2. In a small bowl, stir together the butter and curry powder.
3. Place the sweet potatoes and Brussels sprouts in a large bowl. Drizzle half the curry butter over the vegetables and add the remaining ½ teaspoon of kosher salt. Toss to coat. Transfer the vegetables to the sheet pan and arrange in a single layer around the chicken. Brush half of the remaining curry butter over the chicken.
4. Select AIR ROAST, set temperature to 400°F, and set time to 20 minutes. Select START/PAUSE to begin preheating.
5. Once the unit has preheated, slide the pan into the oven.
6. After 10 minutes, remove the pan from the oven and turn over the chicken thighs. Baste them with the remaining curry butter. Return the pan to the oven and continue cooking.
7. Cooking is complete when the sweet potatoes are tender and the chicken is cooked through and reads 165°F on a meat thermometer.

Oven-Fried Chicken with Smashed Potatoes and Corn

Prep Time: 10 minutes | Cook Time: 25 minutes | Serves 4

- 4 bone-in, skin-on chicken thighs
- 2 teaspoons kosher salt or 1 teaspoon fine salt, divided
- 1 cup Bisquick or similar baking mix
- ½ cup unsalted butter, melted, divided
- 1 pound small red potatoes, quartered
- 3 ears corn, shucked and cut into rounds 1- to 1½-inches thick
- ⅓ cup heavy (whipping) cream
- ½ teaspoon freshly ground black pepper

1. Sprinkle the chicken on all sides with 1 teaspoon of kosher salt. Place the baking mix in a shallow dish. Brush the thighs on all sides with ¼ cup of butter, then dredge them in the baking mix, coating them all on sides. Place the chicken in the center of the sheet pan.
2. Place the potatoes in a large bowl with 2 tablespoons of butter and toss to coat. Place them on one side of the chicken on the pan.
3. Place the corn in a medium bowl and drizzle with the remaining 2 tablespoons of butter. Sprinkle with ¼ teaspoon of kosher salt and toss to coat. Place on the pan on the other side of the chicken.
4. Select AIR ROAST, set temperature to 375°F, and set time to 25 minutes. Select START/PAUSE to begin preheating.
5. Once the unit has preheated, slide the pan into the oven.
6. After 20 minutes, remove the pan from the oven and transfer the potatoes back to the bowl. Return the pan to oven and continue cooking.
7. As the chicken continues cooking, add the cream, black pepper, and remaining ¾ teaspoon of kosher salt to the potatoes. Lightly mash the potatoes with a potato masher or fork.
8. When cooking is complete, the corn will be tender and the chicken cooked through, reading 165°F on a meat thermometer. Remove the pan from the oven and serve the chicken with the smashed potatoes and corn on the side.

Whole Roasted Chicken

Prep Time: 15 minutes | Cook Time: 1 hour | Serves 6

- Olive oil
- 1 teaspoon salt
- 1 teaspoon Italian seasoning
- ½ teaspoon freshly ground black pepper
- ½ teaspoon paprika
- ½ teaspoon garlic powder
- ½ teaspoon onion powder
- 2 tablespoons olive oil
- 1 (4-pound) fryer chicken

1. Spray a fryer basket lightly with olive oil.
2. In a small bowl, mix together the salt, Italian seasoning, pepper, paprika, garlic powder, and onion powder.
3. Remove any giblets from the chicken. Pat the chicken dry very thoroughly with paper towels, including the cavity.
4. Brush the chicken all over with the olive oil and rub it with the seasoning mixture.
5. Truss the chicken or tie the legs with butcher's twine. This will make it easier to flip the chicken during cooking.
6. Place the chicken in the fryer basket, breast side down. Air fry for 30 minutes. Flip the chicken over and baste it with any drippings collected in the bottom drawer of the air fryer. Lightly spray the chicken with olive oil.
7. Air fry for 20 minutes. Flip the chicken over one last time and cook until a thermometer inserted into the thickest part of the thigh reaches at least 165°F and it's crispy and golden, 10 more minutes. Continue to cook, checking every 5 minutes until the chicken reaches the correct internal temperature.
8. Let the chicken rest for 10 minutes before carving.

Chicken Parmesan

Prep Time: 15 minutes | Cook Time: 11 minutes | Serves 4

- 4 chicken tenders
- Italian seasoning
- salt
- ¼ cup cornstarch
- ½ cup Italian salad dressing
- ¼ cup panko breadcrumbs
- ¼ cup grated Parmesan cheese, plus more for serving
- oil for misting or cooking spray
- 8 ounces spaghetti, cooked
- 1 24-ounce jar marinara sauce

1. Pound chicken tenders with meat mallet or rolling pin until about ¼-inch thick.
2. Sprinkle both sides with Italian seasoning and salt to taste.
3. Place cornstarch and salad dressing in 2 separate shallow dishes.
4. In a third shallow dish, mix together the panko crumbs and Parmesan cheese.
5. Dip flattened chicken in cornstarch, then salad dressing. Dip in the panko mixture, pressing into the chicken so the coating sticks well.
6. Spray both sides with oil or cooking spray. Place in air fryer basket in single layer.
7. Cook at 390°F for 5 minutes. Spray with oil again, turning chicken to coat both sides. See tip about turning.
8. Cook for an additional 4 to 6 minutes or until chicken juices run clear and outside is browned.
9. While chicken is cooking, heat marinara sauce and stir into cooked spaghetti.
10. To serve, divide spaghetti with sauce among 4 dinner plates, and top each with a fried chicken tender. Pass additional Parmesan at the table for those who want extra cheese.

Tex-Mex Chicken Stir-Fry

Prep Time: 10 minutes | Cook Time: 20 minutes | Serves 4

- 1 pound low-sodium boneless skinless chicken breasts, cut into 1-inch cubes
- 1 medium onion, chopped
- 1 red bell pepper, chopped
- 1 jalapeño pepper, minced
- 2 teaspoons olive oil
- ⅔ cup canned low-sodium black beans, rinsed and drained (see Tip)
- ½ cup low-sodium salsa
- 2 teaspoons chili powder

1. In a medium metal bowl, mix the chicken, onion, bell pepper, jalapeño, and olive oil. Stir-fry in the air fryer for 10 minutes, stirring once during cooking.
2. Add the black beans, salsa, and chili powder. Cook for 7 to 10 minutes more, stirring once, until the chicken reaches an internal temperature of 165°F on a meat thermometer. Serve immediately.

Crispy Cracked-Pepper Chicken Wings

Prep Time: 15 minutes | Cook Time: 20 minutes | Serves 4

- 1 pound chicken wings
- 3 tablespoons vegetable oil
- ½ cup all-purpose flour
- ½ teaspoon smoked paprika
- ½ teaspoon garlic powder
- ½ teaspoon kosher salt
- 1½ teaspoons freshly cracked black pepper

1. Place the chicken wings in a large bowl. Drizzle the vegetable oil over wings and toss to coat.
2. In a separate bowl, whisk together the flour, paprika, garlic powder, salt, and pepper until combined.
3. Dredge the wings in the flour mixture one at a time, coating them well, and place in the air-fryer basket. Set the air fryer to 400°F for 20 minutes, turning the wings halfway through the cooking time, until the breading is browned and crunchy.

Fennel Chicken

Prep Time: 10 minutes | Cook Time: 30 minutes | Serves 4

- 1½ cup coconut milk
- 2 tbsp. garam masala
- 1½ lb. chicken thighs
- ¾ tbsp. coconut oil, melted

1. Combine the coconut oil and garam masala together in a bowl. Pour the mixture over the chicken thighs and leave to marinate for a half hour.
2. Pre-heat your fryer at 375°F .
3. Cook the chicken into the fryer for fifteen minutes.
4. Add in the coconut milk, giving it a good stir, then cook for an additional ten minutes.
5. Remove the chicken and place on a serving dish. Make sure to pour all of the coconut "gravy" over it and serve immediately.

Chicken Shawarma with Roasted Tomatoes

Prep Time: 10 minutes | Cook Time: 18 minutes | Serves 4

- 1½ pounds boneless, skinless chicken thighs
- 1¼ teaspoon kosher salt or ⅜ teaspoon fine salt, divided
- 2 tablespoons plus 1 teaspoon extra-virgin olive oil, divided
- ⅔ cup plus 2 tablespoons plain Greek yogurt, divided
- 2 tablespoons freshly squeezed lemon juice (about 1 medium lemon)
- 4 garlic cloves, pressed or minced, divided
- 1 generous tablespoon Shawarma Seasoning
- 4 pita breads, cut in half
- 1 pint cherry tomatoes
- ½ small cucumber
- 1 tablespoon chopped fresh parsley

1. Sprinkle the chicken thighs on both sides with 1 teaspoon of kosher salt. Place in a resealable plastic bag and set aside while you make the marinade.
2. In a small bowl, mix together 2 tablespoons of olive oil, 2 tablespoons of yogurt, the lemon juice, 3 pressed garlic cloves, and Shawarma Seasoning until thoroughly combined. Pour the marinade over the chicken. Seal the bag, squeezing out as much air as possible. and massage the chicken to coat the it with the sauce. Set aside.
3. Wrap 2 pita breads each in two pieces of aluminum foil and place on the sheet pan.
4. Select BAKE, set temperature to 300°F, and set time to 6 minutes. Select START/PAUSE to begin preheating.
5. Once the oven has preheated, slide the pan into the oven. After 3 minutes, remove the pan from the oven and turn over the foil packets. Return the pan to the oven and continue cooking. When cooking is complete, remove the pan from the oven and place the foil-wrapped pitas on the top of the oven to keep warm.
6. Remove the chicken from the marinade, letting the excess drip off into the bag. Place them on the sheet pan. Arrange the tomatoes around the sides of the chicken. Discard the marinade.
7. Select AIR BROIL, set temperature to HIGH, and set time to 12 minutes. Select START/PAUSE to begin preheating.
8. Once the unit has preheated, slide the pan into the oven.
9. After 6 minutes, remove the pan from the oven and turn over the chicken. Return the pan to the oven and continue cooking.
10. While the chicken cooks, peel and seed the cucumber. Grate or finely chop it. Wrap it in a paper towel to remove as much moisture as possible. Place the cucumber in a small bowl. Add the remaining ⅔ cup of yogurt, ¼ teaspoon kosher salt, 1 teaspoon of olive oil, 1 pressed garlic clove, and parsley. Whisk until combined.
11. When cooking is complete, the chicken should be browned, crisp along its edges, and sizzling. Remove the pan from the oven and place the chicken on a cutting board. Cut each thigh into several pieces. Unwrap the pitas. Spread a tablespoon or two of sauce into a pita half. Add some chicken and add 2 or 3 roasted tomatoes. Serve.

Turkey Burgers with Cheddar and Roasted Onions

Prep Time: 10 minutes | Cook Time: 25 minutes | Serves 4

- 2 medium yellow or white onions
- 1 tablespoon extra-virgin olive oil or vegetable oil
- 1½ teaspoons kosher salt or ¾ teaspoon fine salt, divided
- 1¼ pound ground turkey
- ⅓ cup mayonnaise
- 1 tablespoon Dijon mustard
- 2 teaspoons Worcestershire sauce
- 4 slices sharp cheddar cheese (about 4 ounces total)
- 4 hamburger buns, sliced

1. Trim the onions and cut them in half through the root. Cut one of the halves in half (so you have a quarter). Grate one quarter. Place the grated onion in a large bowl. Thinly slice the remaining onions and place in a medium bowl with the oil and ½ teaspoon of kosher salt. Toss to coat. Place the onions on the sheet pan in a single layer.
2. Select AIR ROAST, set temperature to 350°F, and set time to 10 minutes. Select START/PAUSE to begin preheating.
3. Once the unit has preheated, slide the pan into the oven.
4. While the onions are cooking, add the turkey to the grated onion. Add the remaining 1 teaspoon of kosher salt, mayonnaise, mustard, and Worcestershire sauce. Mix just until combined, being careful not to overwork the turkey. Divide the mixture into 4 patties, each about ¾-inch thick.
5. When cooking is complete, remove the pan from the oven. Move the onions to one side of the pan and place the burgers on the pan. Poke your finger into the center of each burger to make a deep indentation (this helps the burgers cook evenly).
6. Select AIR BROIL, set temperature to HIGH, and set time to 12 minutes. Select START/PAUSE to begin preheating.
7. Once preheated, slide the pan into the oven. After 6 minutes, remove the pan. Turn the burgers and stir the onions. (If the onions are getting charred, transfer them to a bowl and cover with foil.) Return the pan to the oven and continue cooking. After about 4 minutes, remove the pan and place the cheese slices on the burgers. Return the pan to the oven and continue cooking for about 1 minute, or until the cheese is melted and the center of the burgers has reached at least 160°F on a meat thermometer.
8. When cooking is complete, remove the pan from the oven. Loosely cover the burgers with foil.
9. Lay out the buns, cut-side up, on the oven rack. Select AIR BROIL; set temperature to HIGH, and set time to 3 minutes. Select START/PAUSE to begin. Check the buns after 2 minutes; they should be lightly browned.
10. Remove the buns from the oven. Assemble the burgers and add any condiments you like.

Roasted Chicken

Prep Time: 15 minutes | Cook Time: 75 minutes | Serves 6

- 6 lb. whole chicken
- 1 tsp. olive oil
- 1 tbsp. minced garlic
- 1 white onion, peeled and halved
- 3 tbsp. butter

1. Preheat the fryer at 360°F.
2. Massage the chicken with the olive oil and the minced garlic.
3. Place the peeled and halved onion, as well as the butter, inside of the chicken.
4. Cook the chicken in the fryer for seventy-five minutes.
5. Take care when removing the chicken from the fryer, then carve and serve.

Chicken & Honey Sauce

Prep Time: 5 minutes | Cook Time: 15 minutes | Serves 4

- 4 chicken sausages
- 2 tbsp. honey
- ¼ cup mayonnaise
- 2 tbsp. Dijon mustard
- 1 tbsp. balsamic vinegar
- ½ tsp. dried rosemary

1. Preheat your Air Fryer at 350°F.
2. Place the sausages on the grill pan of your fryer and grill for about 13 minutes, flipping them halfway through the cooking time.
3. In the meantime, make the sauce by whisking together the rest of the ingredients.
4. Pour the sauce over the warm sausages before serving.

Chicken Rochambeau

Prep Time: 15 minutes | Cook Time: 20 minutes | Serves 4

- 1 tablespoon butter
- 4 chicken tenders, cut in half crosswise
- salt and pepper
- ¼ cup flour
- oil for misting
- 4 slices ham, ¼- to ⅜-inches thick and large enough to cover an English muffin
- 2 English muffins, split
- 2 tablespoons butter
- ½ cup chopped green onions
- ½ cup chopped mushrooms
- 2 tablespoons flour
- 1 cup chicken broth
- ¼ teaspoon garlic powder
- 1½ teaspoons Worcestershire sauce

1. Place 1 tablespoon of butter in air fryer baking pan and cook at 390°F for 2 minutes to melt.
2. Sprinkle chicken tenders with salt and pepper to taste, then roll in the ¼ cup of flour.
3. Place chicken in baking pan, turning pieces to coat with melted butter.
4. Cook at 390°F for 5 minutes. Turn chicken pieces over, and spray tops lightly with olive oil. Cook 5 minutes longer or until juices run clear. The chicken will not brown.
5. While chicken is cooking, make the sauce: In a medium saucepan, melt the 2 tablespoons of butter.
6. Add onions and mushrooms and sauté until tender, about 3 minutes.
7. Stir in the flour. Gradually add broth, stirring constantly until you have a smooth gravy.
8. Add garlic powder and Worcestershire sauce and simmer on low heat until sauce thickens, about 5 minutes.
9. When chicken is cooked, remove baking pan from air fryer and set aside.
10. Place ham slices directly into air fryer basket and cook at 390°F for 5 minutes or until hot and beginning to sizzle a little. Remove and set aside on top of the chicken for now.
11. Place the English muffin halves in air fryer basket and cook at 390°F for 1 minute.
12. Open air fryer and place a ham slice on top of each English muffin half. Stack 2 pieces of chicken on top of each ham slice. Cook at 390°F for 1 to 2 minutes to heat through.
13. Place each English muffin stack on a serving plate and top with plenty of sauce.

Chicken Schnitzel Dogs

Prep Time: 15 minutes | Cook Time: 10 minutes | Serves 4

- ½ cup flour
- ½ teaspoon salt
- 1 teaspoon marjoram

- 1 teaspoon dried parsley flakes
- ½ teaspoon thyme
- 1 egg
- 1 teaspoon lemon juice
- 1 teaspoon water
- 1 cup breadcrumbs
- 4 chicken tenders, pounded thin
- oil for misting or cooking spray
- 4 whole-grain hotdog buns
- 4 slices Gouda cheese
- 1 small Granny Smith apple, thinly sliced
- ½ cup shredded Napa cabbage
- coleslaw dressing

1. In a shallow dish, mix together the flour, salt, marjoram, parsley, and thyme.
2. In another shallow dish, beat together egg, lemon juice, and water.
3. Place breadcrumbs in a third shallow dish.
4. Cut each of the flattened chicken tenders in half lengthwise.
5. Dip flattened chicken strips in flour mixture, then egg wash. Let excess egg drip off and roll in breadcrumbs. Spray both sides with oil or cooking spray.
6. Cook at 390°F for 5 minutes. Spray with oil, turn over, and spray other side.
7. Cook for 3 to 5 minutes more, until well done and crispy brown.
8. To serve, place 2 schnitzel strips on bottom of each hotdog bun. Top with cheese, sliced apple, and cabbage. Drizzle with coleslaw dressing and top with other half of bun.

Barbecued Chicken

Prep Time: 10 minutes | Cook Time: 20 minutes | Serves 4

- ⅓ cup no-salt-added tomato sauce
- 2 tablespoons low-sodium grainy mustard
- 2 tablespoons apple cider vinegar
- 1 tablespoon honey
- 2 garlic cloves, minced
- 1 jalapeño pepper, minced
- 3 tablespoons minced onion
- 4 (5-ounce) low-sodium boneless skinless chicken breasts (see Tip)

1. In a small bowl, stir together the tomato sauce, mustard, cider vinegar, honey, garlic, jalapeño, and onion.
2. Brush the chicken breasts with some sauce and grill for 10 minutes.
3. Remove the air fryer basket and turn the chicken; brush with more sauce. Grill for 5 minutes more.
4. Remove the air fryer basket and turn the chicken again; brush with more sauce. Grill for 3 to 5 minutes more, or until the chicken reaches an internal temperature of 165°F on a meat thermometer. Discard any remaining sauce. Serve immediately.

Korean BBQ Beef Bowls

Prep Time: 10 minutes plus 2 hours to marinate | Cook Time: 25 minutes | Serves 4

- ½ cup soy sauce
- 2 tablespoons brown sugar
- 2 tablespoons red wine vinegar or rice vinegar
- 1 tablespoon olive oil, plus more for spraying
- 1 tablespoon sesame oil
- 1 pound flank steak, sliced very thin against the grain
- 2 teaspoons cornstarch
- 2 cups cooked brown rice
- 2 cups steamed broccoli florets

1. In a large bowl, whisk together the soy sauce, brown sugar, vinegar, olive oil, and sesame oil. Add the steak, cover with plastic wrap, and refrigerate for at least 30 minutes or up to 2 hours.
2. Spray a fryer basket lightly with olive oil.
3. Remove as much marinade as possible from the steak. Reserve any leftover marinade.
4. Place the steak in the fryer basket in a single layer. You may need to cook the steak in batches.
5. Air fry for 10 minutes. Flip the steak over and cook until the steak reaches your desired level of doneness, an additional 7 to 10 minutes. The internal temperature should read 125°F for rare, 135°F for medium rare, 145°F for medium, and 150°F for medium well. Transfer the steak to a large bowl and set aside.
6. While the steak is cooking, in a small saucepan over medium-high heat, bring the remaining marinade to a boil.
7. In a small bowl, combine the cornstarch and 1 tablespoon of water to create a slurry. Add the slurry to the marinade, lower the heat to medium-low, and simmer, stirring, until the sauce starts to thicken, a few seconds to 1 minute.
8. Pour the sauce over the steak and stir to combine.
9. To assemble the bowls, spoon ½ cup brown rice and ½ cup of broccoli into each of four bowls and top with the steak.

Beef and Bean Chimichangas

Prep Time: 15 minutes | Cook Time: 15 minutes | Serves 4

- Olive oil
- 1 pound lean ground beef
- 1 tablespoon taco seasoning
- ½ cup salsa
- 1 (16-ounce) can fat-free refried beans
- 4 large whole-wheat tortillas
- ½ cup shredded Cheddar cheese
- 1.Spray fryer basket lightly with olive oil.

1. Spray fryer basket lightly with olive oil.
2. In a large skillet over medium heat, cook the ground beef until browned, about 5 minutes. Add the taco seasoning and salsa and stir to combine. Set aside.
3. Spread ½ cup of refried beans onto each tortilla, leaving a ½ inch border around the edge. Add ¼ of the ground beef mixture to each tortilla and sprinkle with 2 tablespoons of Cheddar cheese.
4. Fold the opposite sides of the tortilla in and roll up.
5. Place the chimichangas in the fryer basket, seam side down. Spray lightly with olive oil. You may need to cook the chimichangas in batches.
6. Air fry until golden brown, 5 to 10 minutes.

Steak Fingers

Prep Time: 15 minutes | Cook Time: 15 minutes | Serves 4

- Olive oil
- ½ cup whole-wheat flour
- 1 teaspoon seasoned salt
- ½ teaspoon freshly ground black pepper
- ¼ teaspoon cayenne pepper
- 2 eggs, beaten
- ½ cup low-fat milk
- 1 pound cube steaks, cut into 1-inch-wide strips

1. Spray a fryer basket lightly with olive oil.
2. In a shallow bowl, mix together the flour, salt, black pepper, and cayenne.
3. In another shallow bowl, whisk together the eggs and milk.
4. Dredge the steak strips in the flour mixture, coat with the egg mixture, and dredge in the flour mixture once more to coat completely.
5. Place the steak strips in the fryer basket in a single layer and spray lightly with olive oil. You may need to cook the steak in batches.
6. Air fry for 8 minutes. Flip the steak strips over and lightly spray with olive oil. Cook until golden brown and crispy, an additional 4 to 7 minutes.

Beef Roll-Ups

Prep Time: 30 minutes plus 30 minutes to marinate | Cook Time: 20 minutes | Serves 4

- 1½ pounds sirloin steak, cut into slices
- 2 tablespoons Worcestershire sauce
- ½ tablespoon garlic powder
- ½ tablespoon onion powder
- 2 medium bell peppers of any color, cut into thin strips
- ½ cup shredded mozzarella cheese
- Salt
- Freshly ground black pepper
- Olive oil

1. Using a meat mallet, pound the steaks very thin.
2. In a small bowl, combine the Worcestershire sauce, garlic powder, and onion powder to make a marinade.
3. Place the steaks and marinade in a large zip-top plastic bag, seal, and refrigerate for at least 30 minutes.
4. Soak 8 toothpicks in water for 15 to 20 minutes.
5. Place ¼ of the bell peppers and ¼ of the mozzarella cheese in the center of each steak. Season with salt and black pepper. Roll each steak up tightly and secure with 2 toothpicks.
6. Spray a fryer basket lightly with olive oil. Place the beef roll-ups in the fryer basket, toothpick side down, in a single layer. You may need to cook the roll-ups in batches.
7. Air fry for 10 minutes. Flip the steaks over and cook until the meat reaches an internal temperature of at least 150°F, an additional 7 to 10 minutes.
8. Let the roll-ups rest for 10 minutes before serving.

Carne Asada

Prep Time: 10 minutes plus 30 minutes to marinate | Cook Time: 8 minutes | Serves 4

- Juice of 2 limes
- 1 orange, peeled and seeded
- 1 cup fresh cilantro leaves
- 1 jalapeño, diced
- 2 tablespoons vegetable oil
- 2 tablespoons apple cider vinegar
- 2 teaspoons ancho chile powder
- 2 teaspoons sugar
- 1 teaspoon kosher salt
- 1 teaspoon cumin seeds
- 1 teaspoon coriander seeds
- 1½ pounds skirt steak, cut into 3 pieces

1. In a blender, combine the lime juice, orange, cilantro, jalapeño, vegetable oil, vinegar, chile powder, sugar, salt, cumin, and coriander. Blend until smooth.
2. Place the steak in a resealable plastic bag. Pour the marinade over the steak and seal the bag. Let stand at room temperature for 30 minutes or cover and refrigerate for up to 24 hours.
3. Place the steak pieces in the air-fryer basket (depending on the size of your air fryer, you may have to do this in two batches). Discard marinade. Set the air fryer to 400°F for 8 minutes. Use a meat thermometer to ensure the steak has reached an internal temperature of 145°F. (It is critical to not overcook skirt steak to avoid toughening the meat.)
4. Transfer the steak to a cutting board and let rest for 10 minutes. Slice across the grain and serve.

Spicy Pork Lettuce Cups

Prep Time: 10 minutes | Cook Time: 12 minutes | Serves 4

- 1 medium pork tenderloin (about 1 pound), silver skin and external fat trimmed
- ⅔ cup Asian-Style Sauce, divided
- 1 teaspoon cornstarch
- 1 medium jalapeño, seeded and minced
- 1 can diced water chestnuts
- ½ large (or 1 very small) red bell pepper, seeded and chopped
- 2 scallions, chopped, white and green parts separated
- 1 head butter lettuce or Boston lettuce
- ½ cup roasted, chopped almonds or peanuts (optional)
- ¼ cup coarsely chopped cilantro (optional)

1. Cut the tenderloin into ¼-inch slices and place them on the sheet pan. Baste with about 3 tablespoons of Asian-Style Sauce. Stir the cornstarch into the remaining sauce and set aside.
2. Select AIR ROAST, set temperature to 375°F, and set time to 12 minutes. Select START/PAUSE to begin preheating.
3. Once the unit has preheated, slide the pan into the oven.
4. After 5 minutes, remove the pan from the oven. Place the pork slices on a cutting board. Place the jalapeño, water chestnuts, red pepper, and the white parts of the scallions on the sheet pan and pour the remaining sauce over. Stir to coat the vegetables with the sauce. Return the pan to the oven and continue cooking.
5. While the vegetables cook, chop the pork into small pieces. Separate the lettuce leaves, discarding any tough outer leaves and setting aside the small inner leaves for another use. You'll want 12 to 18 leaves, depending on size and your appetites.
6. After 5 minutes, remove the pan from the oven. Add the pork to the vegetables, stirring to combine. Return the pan to the oven and continue cooking for the remaining 2 minutes, until the pork is warmed back up and the sauce has reduced slightly.
7. When cooking is complete, remove the pan from the oven. Place the pork and vegetables in a medium serving bowl and stir in half the green parts of the scallions. To serve, spoon some of the pork and vegetables into each of the lettuce leaves. Top with the remaining scallion greens and garnish with the nuts and cilantro (if using).

Italian Sausages with Polenta and Grapes

Prep Time: 10 minutes | Cook Time: 20 minutes | Serves 6

- 2 pounds seedless red grapes
- 3 shallots, sliced
- 2 teaspoons fresh thyme or 1 teaspoon dried thyme
- 2 tablespoons extra-virgin olive oil
- ½ teaspoon kosher salt or ¼ teaspoon fine salt
- Freshly ground black pepper
- 6 links (about 1½ pounds) hot or sweet Italian sausage
- 3 tablespoons sherry vinegar or balsamic vinegar
- 6 (1-inch-thick) slices Oven Polenta or store-bought variety

1. Place the grapes in a large bowl. Add the shallots, thyme, olive oil, salt, and pepper. Gently toss. Place the grapes on the sheet pan. Arrange the sausage links evenly on the pan.
2. Select AIR ROAST, set temperature to 375°F, and set time to 20 minutes. Select START/PAUSE to begin preheating.
3. Once preheated, slide the pan into the oven.
4. After 10 minutes, remove the pan. Turn over the sausages and sprinkle the vinegar over the sausages and grapes. Gently toss the grapes and move them to one side of the pan. Place the polenta slices on the pan. Return the pan to the oven and continue cooking.
5. When cooking is complete, the grapes should be very soft and the sausages browned.

Pork Chops

Prep Time: 5 minutes | Cook Time: 20 minutes | Serves 2

- 2 bone-in, centercut pork chops, 1-inch thick (10 ounces each)
- 2 teaspoons Worcestershire sauce
- salt and pepper
- cooking spray

1. Rub the Worcestershire sauce into both sides of pork chops.
2. Season with salt and pepper to taste.
3. Spray air fryer basket with cooking spray and place the chops in basket side by side.
4. Cook at 360°F for 16 to 20 minutes or until well done. Let rest for 5 minutes before serving.

Beef and Broccoli

Prep Time: 10 minutes | Cook Time: 18 minutes | Serves 4

- 2 tablespoons cornstarch
- ½ cup low-sodium beef broth
- 1 teaspoon low-sodium soy sauce
- 12 ounces sirloin strip steak, cut into 1-inch cubes
- 2½ cups broccoli florets
- 1 onion, chopped
- 1 cup sliced cremini mushrooms (see Tip)
- 1 tablespoon grated fresh ginger
- Brown rice, cooked (optional)

1. In a medium bowl, stir together the cornstarch, beef broth, and soy sauce.
2. Add the beef and toss to coat. Let stand for 5 minutes at room temperature.
3. With a slotted spoon, transfer the beef from the broth mixture into a medium metal bowl. Reserve the broth.
4. Add the broccoli, onion, mushrooms, and ginger to the beef. Place the bowl into the air fryer and cook for 12 to 15 minutes, or until the beef reaches at least 145°F on a meat thermometer and the vegetables are tender.
5. Add the reserved broth and cook for 2 to 3 minutes more, or until the sauce boils.
6. Serve immediately over hot cooked brown rice, if desired.

Pork Cutlets with Aloha Salsa

Prep Time: 20 minutes | Cook Time: 9 minutes | Serves 4

- 1 cup fresh pineapple, chopped in small pieces
- ¼ cup red onion, finely chopped
- ¼ cup green or red bell pepper, chopped
- ½ teaspoon ground cinnamon
- 1 teaspoon low-sodium soy sauce
- ⅛ teaspoon crushed red pepper
- ⅛ teaspoon ground black pepper
- 2 eggs
- 2 tablespoons milk
- ¼ cup flour
- ¼ cup panko breadcrumbs
- 4 teaspoons sesame seeds
- 1 pound boneless, thin pork cutlets (⅜- to ½-inch thick)
- lemon pepper and salt
- ¼ cup cornstarch
- oil for misting or cooking spray

1. In a medium bowl, stir together all ingredients for salsa. Cover and refrigerate while cooking pork.
2. Preheat air fryer to 390°F.
3. Beat together eggs and milk in shallow dish.
4. In another shallow dish, mix together the flour, panko, and sesame seeds.
5. Sprinkle pork cutlets with lemon pepper and salt to taste. Most lemon pepper seasoning contains salt, so go easy adding extra.
6. Dip pork cutlets in cornstarch, egg mixture, and then panko coating. Spray both sides with oil or cooking spray.
7. Cook cutlets for 3 minutes. Turn cutlets over, spraying both sides, and continue cooking for 4 to 6 minutes or until well done.
8. Serve fried cutlets with salsa on the side.

Bulgogi Burgers

Prep Time: 15 minutes plus 30 minutes to marinate | Cook Time: 10 minutes | Serves 4

- 1 pound 85% lean ground beef
- ¼ cup chopped scallions
- 2 tablespoons gochujang (Korean red chile paste)
- 1 tablespoon dark soy sauce
- 2 teaspoons minced garlic
- 2 teaspoons minced fresh ginger
- 2 teaspoons sugar
- 1 tablespoon toasted sesame oil
- ½ teaspoon kosher salt
- ¼ cup mayonnaise
- ¼ cup chopped scallions
- 1 tablespoon gochujang (Korean red chile paste)
- 1 tablespoon toasted sesame oil
- 2 teaspoons sesame seeds
- 4 hamburger buns

1. For the burgers: In a large bowl, mix the ground beef, scallions, gochujang, soy sauce, garlic, ginger, sugar, sesame oil, and salt. Marinate at room temperature for 30 minutes, or cover and refrigerate for up to 24 hours.
2. Divide the meat into four portions and form them into round patties. Make a slight depression in the middle of each patty with your thumb to prevent them from puffing up into a dome shape while cooking.
3. Place the patties in a single layer in the air-fryer basket. Set the air fryer to 350°F for 10 minutes.
4. Meanwhile, for the gochujang mayonnaise: Stir together the mayonnaise, scallions, gochujang, sesame oil, and sesame seeds.
5. At the end of the cooking time, use a meat thermometer to ensure the burgers have reached an internal temperature of 160°F (medium).
6. To serve, place the burgers on the buns and top with the mayonnaise.

Pork Loin

Prep Time: 10 minutes | Cook Time: 50 minutes | Serves 8

- 1 tablespoon lime juice
- 1 tablespoon orange marmalade
- 1 teaspoon coarse brown mustard
- 1 teaspoon curry powder
- 1 teaspoon dried lemongrass
- 2-pound boneless pork loin roast
- salt and pepper
- cooking spray

1. Mix together the lime juice, marmalade, mustard, curry powder, and lemongrass.
2. Rub mixture all over the surface of the pork loin. Season to taste with salt and pepper.
3. Spray air fryer basket with nonstick spray and place pork roast diagonally in basket.
4. Cook at 360°F for approximately 45 to 50 minutes, until roast registers 130°F on a meat thermometer.
5. Wrap roast in foil and let rest for 10 minutes before slicing.

Easy Beef Satay

Prep Time: 10 minutes plus 30minutes to marinate | Cook Time: 8 minutes | Serves 4

- 1 pound beef flank steak, thinly sliced into long strips
- 2 tablespoons vegetable oil
- 1 tablespoon fish sauce
- 1 tablespoon soy sauce
- 1 tablespoon minced fresh ginger
- 1 tablespoon minced garlic
- 1 tablespoon sugar
- 1 teaspoon sriracha or other hot sauce
- 1 teaspoon ground coriander
- ½ cup chopped fresh cilantro
- ¼ cup chopped roasted peanuts
- Easy Peanut Sauce, for serving

1. Place the beef strips in a large bowl or resealable plastic bag. Add the vegetable oil, fish sauce, soy sauce, ginger, garlic, sugar, sriracha, coriander, and ¼ cup of the cilantro to the bag. Seal and massage the bag to thoroughly coat and combine. Marinate at room temperature for 30 minutes, or cover and refrigerate for up to 24 hours.
2. Using tongs, remove the beef strips from the bag and lay them flat in the air-fryer basket, minimizing overlap as much as possible; discard the marinade. Set the air fryer to 400°F for 8 minutes, turning the beef strips halfway through the cooking time.
3. Transfer the meat to a serving platter. Sprinkle with the remaining ¼ cup cilantro and the peanuts. Serve with peanut sauce.

Sausage Cheese Calzone

Prep Time: 30 minutes | Cook Time: 8 minutes per batch | Serves 8

- 2 cups white wheat flour, plus more for kneading and rolling
- 1 package (¼ ounce) RapidRise yeast
- 1 teaspoon salt
- ½ teaspoon dried basil
- 1 cup warm water (115°F to 125°F)
- 2 teaspoons olive oil
- ¼ pound Italian sausage
- ½ cup ricotta cheese
- 4 ounces mozzarella cheese, shredded
- ¼ cup grated Parmesan cheese
- oil for misting or cooking spray
- marinara sauce for serving

1. Crumble Italian sausage into air fryer baking pan and cook at 390°F for 5 minutes. Stir, breaking apart, and cook for 3 to 4 minutes, until well done. Remove and set aside on paper towels to drain.
2. To make dough, combine flour, yeast, salt, and basil. Add warm water and oil and stir until a soft dough forms. Turn out onto lightly floured board and knead for 3 or 4 minutes. Let dough rest for 10 minutes.
3. To make filling, combine the three cheeses in a medium bowl and mix well. Stir in the cooked sausage.
4. Cut dough into 8 pieces.
5. Working with 4 pieces of the dough, press each into a circle about 5 inches in diameter. Top each dough circle with 2 heaping tablespoons of filling. Fold over to create a half-moon shape and press edges firmly together. Be sure that edges are firmly sealed to prevent leakage. Spray both sides with oil or cooking spray.
6. Place 4 calzones in air fryer basket and cook at 360°F for 5 minutes. Mist with oil and cook for 2 to 3 minutes, until crust is done and nicely browned.
7. While the first batch is cooking, press out the remaining dough, fill, and shape into calzones.
8. Spray both sides with oil and cook for 5 minutes. If needed, mist with oil and continue cooking for 2 to 3 minutes longer. This second batch will cook a little faster than the first because your air fryer is already hot.
9. Serve with marinara sauce on the side for dipping.

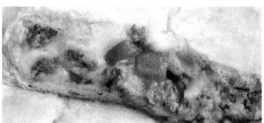

Beef and Fruit Stir-Fry
Prep Time: 15 minutes | Cook Time: 11 minutes | Serves 4

- 12 ounces sirloin tip steak, thinly sliced
- 1 tablespoon freshly squeezed lime juice
- 1 cup canned mandarin orange segments, drained, juice reserved (see Tip)
- 1 cup canned pineapple chunks, drained, juice reserved (see Tip)
- 1 teaspoon low-sodium soy sauce
- 1 tablespoon cornstarch
- 1 teaspoon olive oil
- 2 scallions, white and green parts, sliced
- Brown rice, cooked (optional)

1. In a medium bowl, mix the steak with the lime juice. Set aside.
2. In a small bowl, thoroughly mix 3 tablespoons of reserved mandarin orange juice, 3 tablespoons of reserved pineapple juice, the soy sauce, and cornstarch.
3. Drain the beef and transfer it to a medium metal bowl, reserving the juice. Stir the reserved juice into the mandarin-pineapple juice mixture. Set aside.
4. Add the olive oil and scallions to the steak. Place the metal bowl in the air fryer and cook for 3 to 4 minutes, or until the steak is almost cooked, shaking the basket once during cooking.
5. Stir in the mandarin oranges, pineapple, and juice mixture. Cook for 3 to 7 minutes more, or until the sauce is bubbling and the beef is tender and reaches at least 145°F on a meat thermometer.
6. Stir and serve over hot cooked brown rice, if desired.

Tender Country Ribs
Prep Time: 5 minutes | Cook Time: 25 minutes | Serves 4

- 12 country-style pork ribs, trimmed of excess fat
- 2 tablespoons cornstarch
- 2 tablespoons olive oil
- 1 teaspoon dry mustard
- ½ teaspoon thyme
- ½ teaspoon garlic powder
- 1 teaspoon dried marjoram
- Pinch salt
- Freshly ground black pepper

1. Place the ribs on a clean work surface.
2. In a small bowl, combine the cornstarch, olive oil, mustard, thyme, garlic powder, marjoram, salt, and pepper, and rub into the ribs.
3. Place the ribs in the air fryer basket and roast for 10 minutes.
4. Carefully turn the ribs using tongs and roast for 10 to 15 minutes or until the ribs are crisp and register an internal temperature of at least 150°F.

Burger Patties
Prep Time: 3 minutes | Cook Time: 12 minutes | Serves 6

- 1 lb. ground beef
- 6 cheddar cheese slices
- Pepper and salt to taste

1. Preheat the Air Fryer to 350°F.
2. Sprinkle the salt and pepper on the ground beef.
3. Shape six equal portions of the ground beef into patties and put each one in the Air Fryer basket.
4. Air fry the patties for 10 minutes.
5. Top the patties with the cheese slices and air fry for one more minute.
6. Serve the patties on top of dinner rolls.

Beef Rolls

Prep Time: 5 minutes | Cook Time: 25 minutes | Serves 2

- 2 lb. beef flank steak
- 3 tsp. pesto
- 1 tsp. black pepper
- 6 slices of provolone cheese
- 3 oz. roasted red bell peppers
- ¾ cup baby spinach
- 1 tsp. sea salt

1. Spoon equal amounts of the pesto onto each flank steak and spread it across evenly.
2. Place the cheese, roasted red peppers and spinach on top of the meat, about three-quarters of the way down.
3. Roll the steak up, holding it in place with toothpicks. Sprinkle on the sea salt and pepper.
4. Place inside the Air Fryer and cook for 14 minutes at 400°F, turning halfway through the cooking time.
5. Allow the beef to rest for 10 minutes before slicing up and serving.

Spring Rolls

Prep Time: 15 minutes | Cook Time: 20 minutes | Serves 20

- ⅓ cup noodles
- 1 cup beef minced
- 2 tbsp. cold water
- 1 packet spring roll sheets
- 1 tsp. soy sauce
- 1 cup fresh mix vegetables
- 3 garlic cloves, minced
- 1 small onion, diced
- 1 tbsp. sesame oil

1. Cook the noodle in hot water to soften them up, drain them and snip them to make them shorter.
2. In a frying pan over medium heat, cook the minced beef, soy sauce, mixed vegetables, garlic, and onion in a little oil until the beef minced is cooked through. Take the pan off the heat and throw in the noodles. Mix well to incorporate everything.
3. Unroll a spring roll sheet and lay it flat. Scatter the filling diagonally across it and roll it up, brushing the edges lightly with water to act as an adhesive. Repeat until you have used up all of the sheets and the filling.
4. Pre-heat the Air Fryer to 350°F.
5. Coat each spring roll with a light brushing of oil and transfer to the fryer.
6. Cook for 8 minutes and serve hot.

Chapter 6
Fish and Seafood

Blackened Shrimp Tacos

Prep Time: 10 minutes | Cook Time: 15 minutes | Serves 4

- 1 teaspoon olive oil, plus more for spraying
- 12 ounces medium shrimp, deveined, tails off
- 1 to 2 teaspoons blackened seasoning
- 8 corn tortillas, warmed
- 1 (14-ounce) bag coleslaw mix
- 2 limes, cut in half

1. Spray a fryer basket lightly with olive oil.
2. Dry the shrimp with a paper towel to remove excess water.
3. In a medium bowl, toss the shrimp with 1 teaspoon of olive oil and blackened seasoning.
4. Place the shrimp in the fryer basket and cook for 5 minutes. Shake the basket, lightly spray with olive oil, and cook until the shrimp are cooked through and starting to brown, 5 to 10 more minutes.
5. Fill each tortilla with the coleslaw mix and top with the blackened shrimp. Squeeze fresh lime juice over top.

Chili-Lime Shrimp Bowl

Prep Time: 10 minutes | Cook Time: 15 minutes | Serves 4

- 1 teaspoon olive oil, plus more for spraying
- 2 teaspoons lime juice
- 1 teaspoon honey
- 1 teaspoon minced garlic
- 1 teaspoon chili powder
- Salt
- 12 ounces medium cooked shrimp, thawed, deveined, peeled
- 2 cups cooked brown rice
- 1 (15-ounce) can seasoned black beans, warmed
- 1 large avocado, chopped
- 1 cup sliced cherry tomatoes

1. Spray a fryer basket lightly with olive oil.
2. In a medium bowl, mix together the lime juice, 1 teaspoon of olive oil, honey, garlic, chili powder, and salt to make a marinade.
3. Add the shrimp and toss to coat evenly in the marinade.
4. To assemble the bowls, spoon ¼ of the rice, black beans, avocado, and cherry tomatoes into each of four bowls. Top with the shrimp and serve.

Seasoned Breaded Shrimp

Prep Time: 15 minutes | Cook Time: 15 minutes | Serves 4

- Olive oil
- 2 teaspoons Old Bay seasoning, divided
- ½ teaspoon garlic powder
- ½ teaspoon onion powder
- 1 pound large shrimp, deveined, with tails on
- 2 large eggs
- ½ cup whole-wheat panko bread crumbs

1. Spray a fryer basket lightly with olive oil.
2. In a medium bowl, mix together 1 teaspoon of Old Bay seasoning, garlic powder, and onion powder. Add the shrimp and toss with the seasoning mix to lightly coat.
3. In a separate small bowl whisk the eggs with 1 teaspoon water.
4. In a shallow bowl, mix together the remaining 1 teaspoon Old Bay seasoning and the panko bread crumbs.
5. Dip each shrimp in the egg mixture and dredge in the bread crumb mixture to evenly coat.
6. Air fry until the shrimp is cooked through and crispy, 10 to 15 minutes, shaking the basket at 5-minute intervals to redistribute and evenly cook.

Country Shrimp "Boil"

Prep Time: 10 minutes | Cook Time: 20 minutes | Serves 4

- 2 tablespoons olive oil, plus more for spraying
- 1 pound large shrimp, deveined, tail on
- 1 pound smoked turkey sausage, cut into thick slices
- 2 corn cobs, quartered
- 1 zucchini, cut into bite-sized pieces
- 1 red bell pepper, cut into chunks
- 1 tablespoon Old Bay seasoning

1. Spray the fryer basket lightly with olive oil.
2. In a large bowl, mix together the shrimp, turkey sausage, corn, zucchini, bell pepper, and Old Bay seasoning, and toss to coat with the spices. Add the 2 tablespoons of olive oil and toss again until evenly coated.
3. Spread the mixture in the fryer basket in a single layer. You will need to cook in batches.
4. Air fry until cooked through, 15 to 20 minutes, shaking the basket every 5 minutes for even cooking.

Popcorn Crawfish

Prep Time: 15 minutes | Cook Time: 20 minutes | Serves 4

- ½ cup flour, plus 2 tablespoons
- ½ teaspoon garlic powder
- 1½ teaspoons Old Bay Seasoning
- ½ teaspoon onion powder
- ½ cup beer, plus 2 tablespoons
- 12-ounce package frozen crawfish tail meat, thawed and drained
- oil for misting or cooking spray
- 1½ cups panko crumbs
- 1 teaspoon Old Bay Seasoning
- ½ teaspoon ground black pepper

1. In a large bowl, mix together the flour, garlic powder, Old Bay Seasoning, and onion powder. Stir in beer to blend.
2. Add crawfish meat to batter and stir to coat.
3. Combine the coating ingredients in food processor and pulse to finely crush the crumbs. Transfer crumbs to shallow dish.
4. Preheat air fryer to 390°F.
5. Pour the crawfish and batter into a colander to drain. Stir with a spoon to drain excess batter.
6. Working with a handful of crawfish at a time, roll in crumbs and place on a cookie sheet. It's okay if some of the smaller pieces of crawfish meat stick together.
7. Spray breaded crawfish with oil or cooking spray and place all at once into air fryer basket.
8. Cook at 390°F for 5 minutes. Shake basket or stir and mist again with olive oil or spray. Cook 5 more minutes, shake basket again, and mist lightly again. Continue cooking 3 to 5 more minutes, until browned and crispy.

Citrus Soy Salmon with Sesame Bok Choy & Shiitakes

Prep Time: 15 minutes plus 30 minutes to marinate | Cook Time: 12 minutes | Serves 2

- ½ cup fresh orange juice
- ¼ cup soy sauce
- 3 tablespoons rice vinegar
- 2 garlic cloves, minced
- 1 tablespoon minced fresh ginger
- 1 tablespoon vegetable oil
- 2 teaspoons finely grated orange zest
- ½ teaspoon kosher salt
- 2 (5- to 6-ounce) salmon fillets
- 2 heads baby bok choy, halved lengthwise
- 2 ounces shiitake mushrooms, stemmed
- 1 tablespoon toasted sesame oil
- Kosher salt
- ½ teaspoon sesame seeds, toasted

1. For the fish: In a small bowl, whisk together the orange juice, soy sauce, vinegar, garlic, ginger, vegetable oil, orange zest, and salt. Set aside half the marinade. Place the salmon in a gallon-size resealable bag. Pour the remaining marinade over the salmon. Seal and massage to coat. Let stand at room temperature for 30 minutes.
2. Place the salmon in the air-fryer basket. (Discard marinade.) Set the air fryer to 400°F for 12 minutes.
3. Meanwhile, for the vegetables: Brush the bok choy and mushroom caps all over with the sesame oil and season lightly with salt.
4. After the salmon has cooked for 6 minutes, add the vegetables around the salmon in the air-fryer basket. Cook for the remaining 6 minutes.
5. To serve, drizzle the salmon with some of the reserved marinade and sprinkle the vegetables with the sesame seeds.

Sesame Scallops with Snow Peas and Mushrooms

Prep Time: 10 minutes | Cook Time: 8 minutes | Serves 4

- 1 pound sea scallops
- 3 tablespoons hoisin sauce
- ½ cup toasted sesame seeds
- 6 ounces snow peas, trimmed
- 3 teaspoons vegetable oil, divided
- 1 teaspoon sesame oil
- 1 teaspoon soy sauce
- 1 cup Oven-Roasted Mushrooms

1. With a basting brush, coat the flat sides of the scallops with the hoisin sauce. Place the sesame seeds in a flat dish. Place the coated sides of the scallops in the seeds, pressing them into the scallops to adhere. Repeat with the other sides of the scallops, so both flat sides are coated with hoisin sauce and sesame seeds.
2. In a medium bowl, toss the snow peas with 1 teaspoon of vegetable oil, the sesame oil, and soy sauce.
3. Brush the sheet pan with the remaining 2 teaspoons of vegetable oil. Place the scallops in the center of the pan. Arrange the snow peas in a single layer around the scallops.
4. Select AIR ROAST, set temperature to 375°F, and set time to 8 minutes. Select START/PAUSE to begin preheating.
5. Once the unit has preheated, slide the pan into the oven.
6. After 5 minutes, remove the pan from the oven. Using a small spatula, carefully turn the scallops over. Add the mushrooms to the peas and stir to combine. Return the pan to the oven and continue cooking.
7. When cooking is complete, the peas should be sizzling and the scallops just cooked through. Remove the pan from the oven and serve.

Tilapia Meunière with Green Beans and Potatoes

Prep Time: 10 minutes | Cook Time: 20 minutes | Serves 4

- 10 ounces Yukon Gold potatoes, sliced ¼-inch thick
- 5 tablespoons unsalted butter, melted, divided
- 1 teaspoon kosher salt or ½ teaspoon fine salt, divided
- 4 (8-ounce) tilapia fillets
- ½ pound green beans, trimmed
- Juice of 1 lemon
- 2 tablespoons chopped fresh parsley

1. Place the potatoes in a large bowl. Drizzle with 2 tablespoons of butter and ¼ teaspoon of kosher salt. Place on the sheet pan.
2. Select AIR ROAST, set temperature to 375°F, and set time to 20 minutes. Select START/PAUSE to begin preheating.
3. Once the unit has preheated, slide the pan into the oven.
4. While the potatoes cook, salt the fish fillets on both sides with ½ teaspoon of kosher salt. Place the green beans in the potato bowl and toss with the remaining ¼ teaspoon of kosher salt and 1 tablespoon of butter.
5. After 10 minutes, remove the pan from the oven and move the potatoes to one side. Place the fish fillets in the center of the pan and add the green beans on the other side. Drizzle the fish with 2 tablespoons of butter. Return the pan to the oven and continue cooking.
6. When cooking is complete, the fish should flake apart with a fork. The beans should be tender and starting to crisp. Remove the pan from the oven. To serve, drizzle the lemon juice over the fish, and sprinkle the parsley over the fish and vegetables.

Miso Salmon

Prep Time: 10 minutes | Cook Time: 12 minutes | Serves 2

- 2 tablespoons brown sugar
- 2 tablespoons soy sauce
- 2 tablespoons white miso paste
- 1 teaspoon minced garlic
- 1 teaspoon minced fresh ginger
- ½ teaspoon freshly cracked black pepper
- 2 (5-ounce) salmon fillets
- Vegetable oil spray
- 1 teaspoon sesame seeds
- 2 scallions, thinly sliced, for garnish

1. In a small bowl, whisk together the brown sugar, soy sauce, miso, garlic, ginger, and pepper to combine.
2. Place the salmon fillets on a plate. Pour half the sauce over the fillets; turn the fillets to coat the other sides with sauce.
3. Spray the air-fryer basket with vegetable oil spray. Place the sauce-covered salmon in the basket. Set the air fryer to 400°F for 12 minutes. Halfway through the cooking time, brush additional miso sauce on the salmon.
4. Sprinkle the salmon with the sesame seeds and scallions and serve.

Snapper Veracruz

Prep Time: 9 minutes | Cook Time: 18 minutes | Serves 4

- 2 tablespoons extra-virgin olive oil
- ½ onion, chopped fine (about ½ cup)
- 2 large garlic cloves, minced
- 1 (14.5-ounce) can diced tomatoes, drained
- ½ teaspoon dried oregano
- ¼ cup sliced green olives
- 2 tablespoons chopped fresh parsley, divided
- 3 tablespoons capers, divided
- 4 (6-ounce) snapper fillets
- ½ teaspoon kosher salt or ¼ teaspoon fine salt

1. Pour the olive oil onto the sheet pan. Slide the pan into the oven.
2. Select AIR ROAST, set temperature to 375°F, and set time to 18 minutes. Select START/PAUSE to begin preheating.
3. When unit has preheated, remove the pan from the oven and add the onion and garlic to the oil in the pan. Stir the vegetables to coat with the oil. Return the pan to the oven and continue cooking.
4. After 2 minutes, remove the pan from the oven. Add the tomatoes, oregano, olives, 1 tablespoon of parsley, and 1½ tablespoons of capers. Stir gently to combine. Return the pan to the oven and continue cooking for 6 minutes to heat the sauce through.
5. While the sauce cooks, season the snapper fillets on both sides with the salt.
6. After 6 minutes, remove the pan from the oven.

Place the snapper fillets in the middle of the sheet pan and spoon some of the sauce over the fish. Return the pan to the oven and continue cooking.

7. When cooking is complete, the fish should flake apart with a fork. Remove the pan from the oven and garnish with the remaining 1 tablespoon of parsley and 1½ tablespoons of capers. Serve with steamed rice or warm tortillas, if desired.

Salmon

Prep Time: 35 minutes | Cook Time: 10 minutes | Serves 4

- marinade
- 3 tablespoons low-sodium soy sauce
- 3 tablespoons rice vinegar
- 3 tablespoons ketchup
- 3 tablespoons olive oil
- 3 tablespoons brown sugar
- 1 teaspoon garlic powder
- ½ teaspoon ground ginger
- 4 salmon fillets (½-inch thick, 3 to 4 ounces each)
- cooking spray

1. Mix all marinade ingredients until well blended.
2. Place salmon in sealable plastic bag or shallow container with lid. Pour marinade over fish and turn to coat well. Refrigerate for 30 minutes.
3. Drain marinade, and spray air fryer basket with cooking spray.
4. Place salmon in basket, skin-side down.
5. Cook at 360°F for 8 to 10 minutes, watching closely to avoid overcooking. Salmon is done when just beginning to flake and still very moist.

Chapter 7
Vegetarian Recipes

Sweet and Spicy Broccoli

Prep Time: 10 minutes | Cook Time: 20 minutes | Serves 4

- ½ teaspoon olive oil, plus more for spraying
- 1 pound fresh broccoli, cut into florets
- ½ tablespoon minced garlic
- Salt
- 1½ tablespoons soy sauce
- 1 teaspoon white vinegar
- 2 teaspoons hot sauce or sriracha
- 1½ teaspoons honey
- Freshly ground black pepper

1. Spray a fryer basket lightly with olive oil.
2. In a large bowl, toss the broccoli florets with ½ teaspoon of olive oil and the minced garlic. Season with salt.
3. Place the broccoli in the fryer basket in a single layer. Do not overcrowd the broccoli. You will need to cook this in more than one batch.
4. Air fry until lightly browned and crispy, 15 to 20 minutes, making sure to shake the basket every 5 minutes. Repeat for remaining broccoli.
5. While the broccoli is frying, in a small bowl, whisk together the soy sauce, white vinegar, hot sauce, honey, and black pepper. If the honey doesn't incorporate well, microwave the mixture for 10 to 20 seconds until the honey melts.
6. In a large bowl, toss the cooked broccoli with the sauce mixture. Season with additional salt and pepper, if desired. Serve immediately.

Broccoli Cheese Tots

Prep Time: 20 minutes | Cook Time: 15 minutes | Serves 4

- Olive oil
- 12 ounces frozen broccoli, thawed and drained
- 1 large egg
- 1½ teaspoons minced garlic
- ¼ cup grated Parmesan cheese
- ¼ cup shredded reduced-fat sharp Cheddar cheese
- ⅓ cup seasoned whole-wheat bread crumbs
- Salt
- Freshly ground black pepper

1. Spray the fryer basket lightly with olive oil.
2. Gently squeeze the thawed broccoli to remove any excess liquid.
3. In a food processor, combine the broccoli, egg, garlic, Parmesan cheese, Cheddar cheese, bread crumbs, salt, and pepper and pulse until it resembles a coarse meal.
4. Using a tablespoon, scoop up the broccoli mixture and shape into 24 oval "tater tot" shapes.
5. Place the tots in the fryer basket in a single layer, being careful to space them a little bit apart. Lightly spray the tots with oil. You may need to cook them in batches.
6. Air fry for 6 to 7 minutes. Turn the tots over and cook for an additional 6 to 8 minutes or until lightly browned and crispy.

Brown Rice Fritters

Prep Time: 10 minutes | Cook Time: 10 minutes | Serves 4

- 1 (10 ounce) bag frozen cooked brown rice, thawed
- 1 egg
- 3 tablespoons brown rice flour
- ⅓ cup finely grated carrots
- ⅓ cup minced red bell pepper
- 2 tablespoons minced fresh basil
- 3 tablespoons grated Parmesan cheese
- 2 teaspoons olive oil

1. In a small bowl, combine the thawed rice, egg, and flour and mix to blend.
2. Stir in the carrots, bell pepper, basil, and Parmesan cheese.
3. Form the mixture into 8 fritters and drizzle with the olive oil.
4. Put the fritters carefully into the air fryer basket. Air-fry for 8 to 10 minutes, or until the fritters are golden brown and cooked through.

Classic Pizza Margherita

Prep Time: 15 minutes | Cook Time: 12 minutes | Serves 4

- 1 pound store-bought pizza dough
- 2 tablespoons extra-virgin olive oil, divided
- ½ cup Marinara Sauce or store-bought variety
- 6 ounces shredded mozzarella cheese
- ½ cup coarsely shredded Parmesan cheese (about 1½ ounces)
- 2 large tomatoes, seeded and chopped (about 1½ cups)
- ¼ teaspoon kosher salt or ⅛ teaspoon fine salt
- ¼ cup chopped fresh basil
- 2 teaspoons wine vinegar

1. Punch down the pizza dough to release as much air as possible. Place the dough on the sheet pan and press it out toward the edges. The dough will likely spring back and shrink. Be patient and keep working at it, leaving it alone to relax for a few minutes from time to time. As it stretches, I find it helpful to coat my fingers with 1 tablespoon of olive oil and then poke the dough lightly with my fingertips to keep it from shrinking as much. Don't worry if you can't get it all the way to the pan's edges.
2. Spread the marinara sauce over the dough. You'll be able to see the dough through the sauce in places; you don't want a thick coating. Evenly top the sauce with the mozzarella cheese.
3. Select AIR ROAST, set temperature to 425°F, and set time to 12 minutes. Select START/PAUSE to begin preheating.
4. Once the unit has preheated, slide the pan into the oven.
5. After about 8 minutes, remove the pan from the oven. Sprinkle the Parmesan cheese over the pizza. Return the pan to the oven. Alternatively, if you like a crisp crust, use a pizza peel or cake lifter (or even a very large spatula) to slide the pizza off the pan and directly onto the oven rack. Continue cooking.
6. While the pizza cooks, place the tomatoes in a colander or fine-mesh strainer and sprinkle with the salt. Let them drain for a few minutes, then place in a small bowl. Mix in the remaining 1 tablespoon of olive oil, basil, and vinegar.
7. When cooking is complete, the cheese on top will be lightly browned and bubbling and the crust a deep golden brown. Remove the pizza from the sheet pan, if you haven't already, and place it on a wire rack to cool for a few minutes (a rack will keep the crust from getting soggy as it cools). Distribute the tomato mixture evenly over the pizza, then transfer to a cutting board to slice and serve.

Tart & Spicy Indian Potatoes

Prep Time: 10 minutes | Cook Time: 15 minutes | Serves 4

- 4 cups quartered baby yellow potatoes
- 3 tablespoons vegetable oil
- 1 teaspoon ground turmeric
- 1 teaspoon amchoor (see headnote)
- 1 teaspoon kosher salt
- ¼ teaspoon ground cumin
- ¼ teaspoon ground coriander
- ¼ to ½ teaspoon cayenne pepper
- 1 tablespoon fresh lime or lemon juice
- ¼ cup chopped fresh cilantro or parsley

1. In a large bowl, toss together the potatoes, vegetable oil, turmeric, amchoor, salt, cumin, coriander, and cayenne until the potatoes are well coated.
2. Place the seasoned potatoes in the air-fryer basket. Set the air fryer to 400°F for 15 minutes, or until they are cooked through and tender when pierced with a fork.
3. Transfer the potatoes to a serving platter or bowl. Drizzle with the lime juice and sprinkle with the cilantro before serving.

Chiles Rellenos with Red Chile Sauce

Prep Time: 20 minutes | Cook Time: 20 minutes | Serves 2

- 2 poblano peppers, rinsed and dried
- ⅔ cup thawed frozen or drained canned corn kernels
- 1 scallion, sliced
- 2 tablespoons chopped fresh cilantro
- ½ teaspoon kosher salt
- ¼ teaspoon black pepper
- ⅔ cup grated Monterey Jack cheese
- 3 tablespoons extra-virgin olive oil
- ½ cup finely chopped yellow onion
- 2 teaspoons minced garlic
- 1 (6-ounce) can tomato paste
- 2 tablespoons ancho chile powder
- 1 teaspoon dried oregano
- 1 teaspoon ground cumin
- ½ teaspoon kosher salt
- 2 cups chicken broth
- 2 tablespoons fresh lemon juice
- Mexican crema or sour cream, for serving

1. For the peppers: Place the peppers in the air-fryer basket. Set the air fryer to 400°F for 10 minutes, turning the peppers halfway through the cooking time, until their skins are charred. Transfer the peppers to a resealable plastic bag, seal, and set aside to steam for 5 minutes. Peel the peppers and discard the skins. Cut a slit down the center of each pepper, starting at the stem and continuing to the tip. Remove the seeds, being careful not to tear the chile.
2. In a medium bowl, combine the corn, scallion, cilantro, salt, black pepper, and cheese; set aside.
3. Meanwhile, for the sauce (see Note): In a large skillet, heat the olive oil over medium-high heat. Add the onion and cook, stirring, until tender, about 5 minutes. Add the garlic and cook, stirring, for 30 seconds. Stir in the tomato paste, chile powder, oregano, and cumin, and salt. Cook, stirring, for 1 minute. Whisk in the broth and lemon juice. Bring to a simmer and cook, stirring occasionally, while the stuffed peppers finish cooking.
4. Cut a slit down the center of each poblano pepper, starting at the stem and continuing to the tip. Remove the seeds, being careful not to tear the chile.
5. Carefully stuff each pepper with half the corn mixture. Place the stuffed peppers in a 7-inch round baking pan with 4-inch sides. Place the pan in the air-fryer basket. Set the air fryer to 400°F for 10 minutes, or until the cheese has melted.
6. Transfer the stuffed peppers to a serving platter and drizzle with the sauce and some crema.

Three-Cheese Zucchini and Spinach Rolls

Prep Time: 15 minutes | Cook Time: 18 minutes | Serves 6

- 3 large zucchini
- 2½ teaspoons kosher salt or 1¼ teaspoons fine salt, divided
- 1½ cups cooked chopped spinach
- 1½ cups whole milk ricotta cheese
- ½ cup freshly grated Parmesan cheese
- 1½ cups shredded mozzarella, divided
- 1 large egg, lightly beaten
- 1 teaspoon Italian seasoning or ½ teaspoon each dried basil and oregano
- Freshly ground black pepper
- Cooking oil spray
- 1½ cups Marinara Sauce or store-bought variety

1. Cut off the ends of the zucchini and peel several strips off one side to make a flat base. Use a large Y-shaped peeler or sharp cheese plane to cut long slices about ⅛-inch thick. When you get to a point where you can't get any more slices, set that zucchini aside and start on the next. You need 8 good slices per squash, for a total of 24 slices (a few extra never hurts). Save the rest of the zucchini pieces for another recipe, such as the Ratatouille Casserole.
2. Salt one side of the zucchini slices with 1 teaspoon of kosher salt. Place the slices salted-side down on a rack placed over a baking sheet. Salt the other sides with another teaspoon of kosher salt. Let the slices sit for 10 minutes, or until they start to exude water (you'll see it beading up on the surface of the slices and dripping onto the baking sheet).
3. While the zucchini sits, in a medium bowl, combine the spinach, ricotta, Parmesan cheese, ¾ cup of mozzarella, egg, Italian seasoning, remaining ½ teaspoon of kosher salt, and pepper.
4. Spray the sheet pan with cooking oil spray.
5. Rinse the zucchini slices off and blot them dry with a paper towel. Spread about 2 tablespoons of the ricotta mixture evenly along each zucchini slice. Roll up the slice and place each seam-side down on the prepared sheet pan. Place the rolls so they touch, working from the center of the pan out toward the edges. Repeat with remaining zucchini slices and filling. Top the rolls with the marinara sauce and sprinkle with the remaining ¾ cup of mozzarella.
6. Select AIR ROAST, set temperature to 375°F, and set time to 18 minutes. Select START/PAUSE to begin preheating.
7. Once the unit has preheated, slide the pan into the oven.
8. After about 15 minutes, check the rolls. They are done when the cheese is melted and beginning to brown, and the filling is bubbling. If necessary, continue cooking for another 3 to 4 minutes.
9. When cooking is complete, remove the pan from the oven. Serve.

Simple Roasted Cauliflower

Prep Time: 10 minutes | Cook Time: 20 minutes | Serves 4

- Olive oil
- 1 large head cauliflower, broken into small florets
- 2 teaspoons smoked paprika
- 1 teaspoon garlic powder
- Salt
- Freshly ground black pepper

1. Spray a fryer basket lightly with olive oil.
2. In a large bowl, toss the cauliflower florets with the smoked paprika and garlic powder until well coated. Season with salt and pepper.
3. Put the cauliflower in the fryer basket. Lightly spray the florets with oil. You may need to cook them in batches.
4. Air fry until nicely browned and lightly crispy, 20 minutes, shaking the basket every 5 minutes. Serve hot.

Cheese Ravioli

Prep Time: 10 minutes | Cook Time: 11 minutes | Serves 4

- 1 egg
- ¼ cup milk
- 1 cup breadcrumbs
- 2 teaspoons Italian seasoning
- ⅛ teaspoon ground rosemary
- ¼ teaspoon basil
- ¼ teaspoon parsley
- 9-ounce package uncooked cheese ravioli
- ¼ cup flour
- oil for misting or cooking spray

1. Preheat air fryer to 390°F.
2. In a medium bowl, beat together egg and milk.
3. In a large plastic bag, mix together the breadcrumbs, Italian seasoning, rosemary, basil, and parsley.
4. Place all the ravioli and the flour in a bag or a bowl with a lid and shake to coat.
5. Working with a handful at a time, drop floured ravioli into egg wash. Remove ravioli, letting excess drip off, and place in bag with breadcrumbs.
6. When all ravioli are in the breadcrumbs' bag, shake well to coat all pieces.
7. Dump enough ravioli into air fryer basket to form one layer. Mist with oil or cooking spray. Dump the remaining ravioli on top of the first layer and mist with oil.
8. Cook for 5 minutes. Shake well and spray with oil. Break apart any ravioli stuck together and spray any spots you missed the first time.
9. Cook 4 to 6 minutes longer, until ravioli puff up and are crispy golden brown.

Spiced Balsamic Asparagus

Prep Time: 15 minutes | Cook Time: 10 minutes | Serves 4

- 4 tablespoons olive oil, plus more for spraying
- 4 tablespoons balsamic vinegar
- 1½ pounds asparagus, trimmed
- Salt
- Freshly ground black pepper

1. Spray a fryer basket lightly with olive oil.
2. In a medium shallow bowl, whisk together the 4 tablespoons of olive oil and balsamic vinegar to make a marinade.
3. Lay the asparagus in the bowl so they are completely covered by the oil and vinegar mixture and let marinate for 5 minutes.
4. Place the asparagus in a single layer in the air fryer and sprinkle with salt and pepper. You may need to cook them in batches.
5. Air fry for 5 minutes. Shake the basket and cook until the asparagus is tender and lightly browned, 3 to 5 more minutes.

Egg Rolls

Prep Time: 20 minutes | Cook Time: 8 minutes | Serves 4

- 1 clove garlic, minced
- 1 teaspoon sesame oil
- 1 teaspoon olive oil
- ½ cup chopped celery
- ½ cup grated carrots
- 2 green onions, chopped
- 2 ounces mushrooms, chopped
- 2 cups shredded Napa cabbage
- 1 teaspoon low-sodium soy sauce
- 1 teaspoon cornstarch
- salt
- 1 egg
- 1 tablespoon water
- 4 egg roll wraps
- olive oil for misting or cooking spray

1. In a large skillet, sauté garlic in sesame and olive oils over medium heat for 1 minute.
2. Add celery, carrots, onions, and mushrooms to skillet. Cook 1 minute, stirring.
3. Stir in cabbage, cover, and cook for 1 minute or just until cabbage slightly wilts.
4. In a small bowl, mix soy sauce and cornstarch. Stir into vegetables to thicken. Remove from heat. Salt to taste if needed.
5. Beat together egg and water in a small bowl.
6. Divide filling into 4 portions and roll up in egg roll wraps. Brush all over with egg wash to seal.
7. Mist egg rolls very lightly with olive oil or cooking spray and place in air fryer basket.
8. Cook at 390°F for 4 minutes. Turn over and cook 3 to 4 more minutes, until golden brown and crispy.

Roasted Potato Salad

Prep Time: 5 minutes | Cook Time: 25 minutes | Serves 4

- 2 pounds tiny red or creamer potatoes, cut in half
- 1 tablespoon plus ⅓ cup olive oil
- Pinch salt
- Freshly ground black pepper
- 1 red bell pepper, chopped
- 2 green onions, chopped
- ⅓ cup lemon juice
- 3 tablespoons Dijon or yellow mustard

1. Place the potatoes in the air fryer basket and drizzle with 1 tablespoon of the olive oil. Sprinkle with salt and pepper.
2. Roast for 25 minutes, shaking twice during cooking time, until the potatoes are tender and light golden brown.
3. Meanwhile, place the bell pepper and green onions in a large bowl.
4. In a small bowl, combine the remaining ⅓ cup of olive oil, the lemon juice, and mustard, and mix well with a whisk.
5. When the potatoes are cooked, add them to the bowl with the bell peppers and top with the dressing. Toss gently to coat.
6. Let cool for 20 minutes. Stir gently again and serve or refrigerate and serve later.

Indian Okra

Prep Time: 10 minutes | Cook Time: 15 minutes | Serves 4

- About 1 pound okra, sliced ¼ inch thick (4 cups)
- 1 cup coarsely chopped red onion
- 2 tablespoons vegetable oil
- 1 teaspoon ground turmeric
- 1 teaspoon kosher salt
- 1 teaspoon ground cumin
- 1 teaspoon ground coriander
- ¼ to ½ teaspoon cayenne pepper
- ¼ teaspoon amchoor (see recipe; optional)
- ½ cup chopped fresh tomato
- Juice of 1 lemon
- ¼ cup chopped fresh cilantro or parsley

1. In a large bowl, combine the okra and onion. Drizzle with the vegetable oil and sprinkle with the turmeric, salt, cumin, coriander, cayenne, and amchoor (if using).
2. Spread the spiced vegetables over the air-fryer basket, making as even and flat a layer as possible. Set the air fryer to 375°F for 15 minutes, stirring halfway through the cooking time. (Don't panic if you see some stickiness to the okra. This will dissipate once it cooks.) After 10 minutes, add the tomato to the basket. Cook for the remaining 5 minutes, until the tomato is wilted and cooked through.
3. Drizzle the vegetables with the lemon juice and toss to combine. Garnish with the cilantro and serve.

Chapter 8
Desserts and Staples

Gluten-Free Spice Cookies

Prep Time: 10 minutes | Cook Time: 12 minutes | Serves 4

- 4 tablespoons (½ stick) unsalted butter, at room temperature
- 2 tablespoons agave nectar
- 1 large egg
- 2 tablespoons water
- 2½ cups almond flour
- ⅓ cup sugar
- 2 teaspoons ground ginger
- 1 teaspoon ground cinnamon
- ½ teaspoon freshly grated nutmeg
- 1 teaspoon baking soda
- ¼ teaspoon kosher salt

1. Line the bottom of the air-fryer basket with parchment paper cut to fit.
2. In a large bowl using a hand mixer, beat together the butter, agave, egg, and water on medium speed until light and fluffy.
3. Add the almond flour, sugar, ginger, cinnamon, nutmeg, baking soda, and salt. Beat on low speed until well combined.
4. Roll the dough into 2-tablespoon balls and arrange them on the parchment paper in the basket. (They don't really spread too much, but try to leave a little room between them.) Set the air fryer to 325°F for 12 minutes, or until the tops of cookies are lightly browned.
5. Transfer to a wire rack and let cool completely. Store in an airtight container for up to a week.

Red Enchilada Sauce

Prep Time: 15 minutes | Cook Time: 0 minutes | Serves 2 cups

- 3 large ancho chiles, stems and seeds removed, torn into pieces
- 1½ cups very hot water
- 2 garlic cloves, peeled and lightly smashed
- 2 teaspoons kosher salt or 1 teaspoon fine salt
- ½ teaspoon dried oregano
- ½ teaspoon ground cumin
- 1½ teaspoons sugar
- 2 tablespoons wine vinegar

1. Place the chile pieces in the hot water and let sit for 10 to 15 minutes.
2. Pour the chiles and water into a blender jar and add the garlic, salt, oregano, cumin, sugar, and vinegar. Blend until smooth.

Macaroon Bites

Prep Time: 10 minutes | Cook Time: 20 minutes | Serves 2

- 4 egg whites
- ½ tsp vanilla
- ½ tsp EZ-Sweet (or equivalent of 1 cup artificial sweetener)
- 4½ tsp water
- 1 cup unsweetened coconut

1. Preheat your fryer to 375°F/190°C.
2. Combine the egg whites, liquids and coconut.
3. Put into the fryer and reduce the heat to 325°F/160°C.
4. Bake for 15 minutes.
5. Serve!

Gingerbread

Prep Time: 5 minutes | Cook Time: 20 minutes | Serves 6

- cooking spray
- 1 cup flour
- 2 tablespoons sugar
- ¾ teaspoon ground ginger
- ¼ teaspoon cinnamon
- 1 teaspoon baking powder
- ½ teaspoon baking soda
- ⅛ teaspoon salt
- 1 egg
- ¼ cup molasses
- ½ cup buttermilk
- 2 tablespoons oil
- 1 teaspoon pure vanilla extract

1. Preheat air fryer to 330°F.
2. Spray 6 x 6-inch baking dish lightly with cooking spray.
3. In a medium bowl, mix together all the dry ingredients.
4. In a separate bowl, beat the egg. Add molasses, buttermilk, oil, and vanilla and stir until well mixed.
5. Pour liquid mixture into dry ingredients and stir until well blended.
6. Pour batter into baking dish and cook at 330°F for 20 minutes or until toothpick inserted in center of loaf comes out clean.

Apple-Blueberry Hand Pies

Prep Time: 20 minutes | Cook Time: 9 minutes | Serves 4

- 1 medium Granny Smith apple, peeled and finely chopped
- ½ cup dried blueberries
- 1 tablespoon freshly squeezed orange juice
- 1 tablespoon packed brown sugar
- 2 teaspoons cornstarch
- 4 sheets frozen phyllo dough, thawed
- 8 teaspoons unsalted butter, melted
- 8 teaspoons sugar
- Nonstick cooking spray, for coating the phyllo dough

1. In a medium bowl, mix the apple, blueberries, orange juice, brown sugar, and cornstarch.
2. Place 1 sheet of phyllo dough on a work surface with the narrow side facing you. Brush very lightly with 1 teaspoon of butter and sprinkle with 1 teaspoon of sugar. Fold the phyllo sheet in half from left to right.
3. Place one-fourth of the fruit filling at the bottom of the sheet in the center. Fold the left side of the sheet over the filling. Spray lightly with cooking spray. Fold the right side of the sheet over the filling. Brush with 1 teaspoon of butter and sprinkle with 1 teaspoon of sugar.
4. Fold the bottom right corner of the dough up to meet the left side of the pastry sheet to form a triangle. Continue folding the triangles over to enclose the filling, as you would fold a flag. Seal the edge with a bit of water. Spray lightly with cooking spray. Repeat with the remaining 3 sheets of the phyllo, butter, sugar, and cooking spray, making four pies.
5. Place the pies in the air fryer basket. Bake for 7 to 9 minutes, or until golden brown and crisp. Remove the pies and let cool on a wire rack before serving.

Oatmeal-Carrot Cookie Cups

Prep Time: 10 minutes | Cook Time: 10 minutes | Serves 16 cups

- 3 tablespoons unsalted butter, at room temperature
- ¼ cup packed brown sugar
- 1 tablespoon honey
- 1 egg white
- ½ teaspoon vanilla extract
- ⅓ cup finely grated carrot (see Tip)
- ½ cup quick-cooking oatmeal
- ⅓ cup whole-wheat pastry flour
- ½ teaspoon baking soda
- ¼ cup dried cherries

1. In a medium bowl, beat the butter, brown sugar, and honey until well combined.
2. Add the egg white, vanilla, and carrot. Beat to combine.
3. Stir in the oatmeal, pastry flour, and baking soda.
4. Stir in the dried cherries.
5. Double up 32 mini muffin foil cups to make 16 cups. Fill each with about 4 teaspoons of dough. Bake the cookie cups, 8 at a time, for 8 to 10 minutes, or until light golden brown and just set. Serve warm.

Big Chocolate Chip Cookie

Prep Time: 7 minutes | Cook Time: 9 minutes | Serves 4

- Nonstick baking spray with flour
- 3 tablespoons softened butter
- ⅓ cup plus 1 tablespoon brown sugar
- 1 egg yolk
- ½ cup flour
- 2 tablespoons ground white chocolate
- ¼ teaspoon baking soda
- ½ teaspoon vanilla
- ¾ cup chocolate chips

1. In medium bowl, beat the butter and brown sugar together until fluffy. Stir in the egg yolk.
2. Add the flour, white chocolate, baking soda, and vanilla, and mix well. Stir in the chocolate chips.
3. Line a 6-by-6-by-2-inch baking pan with parchment paper. Spray the parchment paper with nonstick baking spray with flour.
4. Spread the batter into the prepared pan, leaving a ½-inch border on all sides.
5. Bake for about 9 minutes or until the cookie is light brown and just barely set.
6. Remove the pan from the air fryer and let cool for 10 minutes. Remove the cookie from the pan, remove the parchment paper, and let cool on a wire rack.

Choco-Coconut Pudding

Prep Time: 5 minutes | Cook Time: 3 minutes plus 1 hour to freeze| Serves 4

- 1 cup coconut milk
- 2 tbsp cacao powder or organic cocoa
- ½ tsp Sugar powder extract or 2 tbsp honey/maple syrup
- ½ tbsp quality gelatin
- 1 tbsp water

1. On a medium heat, combine the coconut milk, cocoa and sweetener.
2. In a separate bowl, mix in the gelatin and water.
3. Add to the pan and stir until fully dissolved.
4. Pour into small dishes and refrigerate for 1 hour.
5. Serve!

Grilled Pineapple Dessert

Prep Time: 5 minutes | Cook Time: 12 minutes | Serves 4

- oil for misting or cooking spray
- 4 ½-inch-thick slices fresh pineapple, core removed
- 1 tablespoon honey
- ¼ teaspoon brandy
- 2 tablespoons slivered almonds, toasted
- vanilla frozen yogurt or coconut sorbet

1. Spray both sides of pineapple slices with oil or cooking spray. Place on grill plate or directly into air fryer basket.
2. Cook at 390°F for 6 minutes. Turn slices over and cook for an additional 6 minutes.
3. Mix together the honey and brandy.
4. Remove cooked pineapple slices from air fryer, sprinkle with toasted almonds, and drizzle with honey mixture.
5. Serve with a scoop of frozen yogurt or sorbet on the side.

Peach Cobbler

Prep Time: 15 minutes | Cook Time: 14 minutes | Serves 4

- 16 ounces frozen peaches, thawed, with juice (do not drain)
- 6 tablespoons sugar
- 1 tablespoon cornstarch
- 1 tablespoon water
- ½ cup flour
- ¼ teaspoon salt
- 3 tablespoons butter
- 1½ tablespoons cold water
- ¼ teaspoon sugar

1. Place peaches, including juice, and sugar in air fryer baking pan. Stir to mix well.
2. In a small cup, dissolve cornstarch in the water. Stir into peaches.
3. In a medium bowl, combine the flour and salt. Cut in butter using knives or a pastry blender. Stir in the cold water to make a stiff dough.
4. On a floured board or wax paper, pat dough into a square or circle slightly smaller than your air fryer baking pan. Cut diagonally into 4 pieces.
5. Place dough pieces on top of peaches, leaving a tiny bit of space between the edges. Sprinkle very lightly with sugar, no more than about ¼ teaspoon.
6. Cook at 360°F for 12 to 14 minutes, until fruit bubbles and crust browns.

Fried Oreos

Prep Time: 7 minutes | Cook Time: 6 minutes per batch | Serves 12 cookies

- oil for misting or nonstick spray
- 1 cup complete pancake and waffle mix
- 1 teaspoon vanilla extract
- ½ cup water, plus 2 tablespoons
- 12 Oreos or other chocolate sandwich cookies
- 1 tablespoon confectioners' sugar

1. Spray baking pan with oil or nonstick spray and place in basket.
2. Preheat air fryer to 390°F.
3. In a medium bowl, mix together the pancake mix, vanilla, and water.
4. Dip 4 cookies in batter and place in baking pan.
5. Cook for 6 minutes, until browned.
6. Repeat steps 4 and 5 for the remaining cookies.
7. Sift sugar over warm cookies.

Chocolate Peanut Butter Cups

Prep Time: 5 minutes | Cook Time: 3 minutes plus 60 minutes to freeze| Serves 2

- 1 stick unsalted butter
- 1 oz / 1 cube unsweetened chocolate
- 5 packets Sugar in the Raw
- 4 tbsp peanut butter

1. In a microwave, melt the butter and chocolate.
2. Add the Sugar.
3. Stir in the cream and peanut butter.
4. Line the muffin tins. Fill the muffin cups.
5. Freeze for 60 minutes.
6. Serve!

Choco-berry Fudge Sauce

Prep Time: 3 minutes | Cook Time: 3 minutes plus 20 minutes to freeze | Serves 2

- 4 oz cream cheese, softened
- 1-3.5 oz 90% chocolate Lindt bar, chopped
- ¼ cup powdered erythritol
- ¼ cup heavy cream
- 1 tbsp Monin sugar-free raspberry syrup

1. In a large skillet, melt together the cream cheese and chocolate.
2. Stir in the sweetener.
3. Remove from the heat and allow to cool.
4. Once cool, mix in the cream and syrup.
5. Serve!

Berry Layer Cake

Prep Time: 8 minutes | Cook Time: 0 minutes | Serves 1

- ¼ lemon pound cake
- ¼ cup whipping cream
- ½ tsp Truvia
- 1/8 tsp orange flavor
- 1 cup of mixed berries

1. Using a sharp knife, divide the lemon cake into small cubes.
2. Dice the strawberries.
3. Combine the whipping cream, Truvia, and orange flavor.
4. Layer the fruit, cake and cream in a glass.
5. Serve!

Chocolate Pudding

Prep Time: 15 minutes plus 30 minutes to freeze | Cook Time: 0 minutes | Serves 1

- 3 tbsp chia seeds
- 1 cup unsweetened milk
- 1 scoop cocoa powder
- ¼ cup fresh raspberries
- ½ tsp honey

1. Mix together all of the ingredients in a large bowl.
2. Let rest for 15 minutes but stir halfway through.
3. Stir again and refrigerate for 30 minutes. Garnish with raspberries.
4. Serve!

Appendix 1 Measurement Conversion Chart

Volume Equivalents (Dry)	
US STANDARD	**METRIC (APPROXIMATE)**
1/8 teaspoon	0.5 mL
1/4 teaspoon	1 mL
1/2 teaspoon	2 mL
3/4 teaspoon	4 mL
1 teaspoon	5 mL
1 tablespoon	15 mL
1/4 cup	59 mL
1/2 cup	118 mL
3/4 cup	177 mL
1 cup	235 mL
2 cups	475 mL
3 cups	700 mL
4 cups	1 L

Weight Equivalents	
US STANDARD	**METRIC (APPROXIMATE)**
1 ounce	28 g
2 ounces	57 g
5 ounces	142 g
10 ounces	284 g
15 ounces	425 g
16 ounces (1 pound)	455 g
1.5 pounds	680 g
2 pounds	907 g

Volume Equivalents (Liquid)		
US STANDARD	**US STANDARD (OUNCES)**	**METRIC (APPROXIMATE)**
2 tablespoons	1 fl.oz.	30 mL
1/4 cup	2 fl.oz.	60 mL
1/2 cup	4 fl.oz.	120 mL
1 cup	8 fl.oz.	240 mL
1 1/2 cup	12 fl.oz.	355 mL
2 cups or 1 pint	16 fl.oz.	475 mL
4 cups or 1 quart	32 fl.oz.	1 L
1 gallon	128 fl.oz.	4 L

Temperatures Equivalents	
FAHRENHEIT(F)	**CELSIUS(C) APPROXIMATE)**
225 °F	107 °C
250 °F	120 ° °C
275 °F	135 °C
300 °F	150 °C
325 °F	160 °C
350 °F	180 °C
375 °F	190 °C
400 °F	205 °C
425 °F	220 °C
450 °F	235 °C
475 °F	245 °C
500 °F	260 °C

Appendix 2 The Dirty Dozen and Clean Fifteen

The Environmental Working Group (EWG) is a nonprofit, nonpartisan organization dedicated to protecting human health and the environment Its mission is to empower people to live healthier lives in a healthier environment. This organization publishes an annual list of the twelve kinds of produce, in sequence, that have the highest amount of pesticide residue-the Dirty Dozen-as well as a list of the fifteen kinds ofproduce that have the least amount of pesticide residue-the Clean Fifteen.

THE DIRTY DOZEN	
The 2016 Dirty Dozen includes the following produce. These are considered among the year's most important produce to buy organic:	
Strawberries	Spinach
Apples	Tomatoes
Nectarines	Bell peppers
Peaches	Cherry tomatoes
Celery	Cucumbers
Grapes	Kale/collard greens
Cherries	Hot peppers
The Dirty Dozen list contains two additional itemskale/collard greens and hot peppers-because they tend to contain trace levels of highly hazardous pesticides.	

THE CLEAN FIFTEEN	
The least critical to buy organically are the Clean Fifteen list. The following are on the 2016 list:	
Avocados	Papayas
Corn	Kiw
Pineapples	Eggplant
Cabbage	Honeydew
Sweet peas	Grapefruit
Onions	Cantaloupe
Asparagus	Cauliflower
Mangos	
Some of the sweet corn sold in the United States are made from genetically engineered (GE) seedstock. Buy organic varieties of these crops to avoid GE produce.	

Appendix 3 Index

VIRGINIA B. SHIVER

Printed in Great Britain
by Amazon

21118055R00045